KT-559-763

SuperBusiness

How I Started SuperJam from My Gran's Kitchen

Fraser Doherty

CAPSTONE

This edition first published 2011

Registered office
Capstone Publishing Ltd. (A Wiley Company), The Atrium, Southern Gate, Chichester, West Sussex, PO19 8SQ, United Kingdom

For details of our global editorial offices, for customer services and for information about how to apply for permission to reuse the copyright material in this book please see our website at www.wiley.com.

Library of Congress Cataloguing-in-Publication Data

9780857081421 (paperback), 9780857081667 (epub), 9780857081674 (emobi), 9780857082152 (epdf)

A catalogue record for this book is available from the British Library.

Set in 11.5/14.5 pt Calibri by Toppan Best-set Premedia Limited

Printed and Bound in the UK by TJ International Ltd, Padstow, Cornwall

Contents

About the 'Jam Boy'

At 22, Fraser Doherty is one of the UK's most successful young entrepreneurs. He started his company, SuperJam, at the age of just 14 using his Gran's jam recipes. By 17, he had become the youngest ever supplier to a major UK supermarket, when Waitrose launched his range of 100% fruit jams in all of its stores. SuperJam is a fun and exciting brand that has reinvigorated the world of jam.

Fraser was named the Global Student Entrepreneur of the Year in 2007, the first ever winner from outside North America. His story is an inspiration to anyone thinking of starting a business. His company, started as a hobby in his parents' tiny kitchen in Scotland, has grown to become a well-loved and iconic brand, stocked by Tesco and Asda Wal-Mart, some of the largest supermarkets in the world.

Named one of the '30 under 30' entrepreneurs in the world by *Inc.* magazine, Fraser's approach to business is one of adventure, of challenging the status quo in a 200-year-old industry, of having fun and investing profits in charitable causes, like hosting massive parties for elderly people.

Acknowledgments

Before I tell you my story, there are a number of people I ought to thank for making it all possible. Not least, of course, my Gran, for teaching me how to make jam in the first place and inspiring the work that I do with the elderly. It has to be said that I'm thankful she's unaware of her intellectual property rights ...

My parents and brother Connor, for letting me cook jam for years on end in their tiny kitchen and supporting me over all these years. But I'd have to say that the best help and support I've had in getting my business off the ground has been from all of the people who believed in my idea and were willing to give me help along the way.

Kevin, my mentor, for sharing the lessons he had learned in setting up his company. Mike, the buyer at Waitrose, for being willing to listen to my ideas and giving me feedback on how to improve them. Simon, the designer, for creating the brand. And the Prince's Trust (the PSYBT), for giving me a small loan in the beginning to get everything started.

Without all of you, none of this would have happened. Thank you for believing in my dream.

My Adventures in Jam

If I were to meet the 14-year-old me and tell him what was in store, he would never believe it. That his tiny enterprise, started with just £5 worth of fruit, would one day be supplying Wal-Mart. He would be terrified and amazed by the thought that one day he would be invited to the most prestigious universities in the world—Columbia, Oxford and dozens of others—to share his story with other young people who dream of starting their own companies.

My story so far is an eight-year adventure that started with a eureka moment in my Gran's tiny kitchen in Glasgow, which ended up giving birth to an internationally loved brand of jam on sale on the shelves of the worlds' largest supermarket chains.

There have been incredible highlights. I have been invited to Downing Street to have dinner with the Prime Minister, after he heard about my story, and I have even seen SuperJam entered into the National Museum of Scotland as an example of an iconic Scottish Brand, alongside Irn-Bru, Baxters and Tunnock's Tea Cakes.

We've celebrated selling our millionth jar, and celebrated many more since. We've launched a cookbook and an iPhone app, sharing my Gran's and my jam-making secrets with the world. The story of SuperJam itself has travelled far and wide, been the feature of television documentaries, school textbooks in Russia and news broadcasts in China. I have found myself sharing my story in places I would never have even of dreamed of finding myself.

SuperJam challenges established brands in an industry that has been around for hundreds of years. It reinvents what jam is: rather than being sickly sweet and made without much fruit, I have created a product that is healthier, more natural and a great deal more ethical than anything that came before it in the world of preserves. It is made 100% from fruit and all natural, and I have had hundreds of letters from people thanking me for coming up with a healthier kind of jam.

Building SuperJam into a commercially successful business has given me the priceless opportunity to help others in my community. For the past couple of years we have been running our own registered charity, The SuperJam Tea Parties, organizing hundreds of free tea dances in community centres and schools for elderly people who live alone or in care. Thousands of people have come along and had a great time and, for me, doing things like that is immensely more satisfying that just running a business to get rich.

My proudest moment of all, though, has to be the day I was lucky enough to share the front page of the Susan Boyle

Special Edition of *The Sun*, when we gave away a jar of SuperJam to all of the paper's 5.5 million readers!

There have also been huge challenges along the way. Convincing massive companies to take me seriously, to risk hundreds of thousands of pounds on my idea, was not easy—not only because I was so young, but because I had no experience and, coming from a hard-working but not very well-off family, absolutely no money behind me.

The process of getting my idea off the ground involved creating a brand that looked as good as it tasted, and then finding a factory that believed in my product enough to put it into production and lend me hundreds of thousands of pounds. Oh, and once that was done, I had to figure out how to convince supermarket buyers to stock my product, alongside the tried-and-tested brands that have been on sale for 100 years or more.

I wanted to write this book to share with you the adventure that I have been on over the past few years, the ups and downs, things I found fun and lessons I have learned. I felt that the time has come to share the SuperJam story with you, now that the company is no longer a tiny start-up but an established brand that has had massive success in the major supermarkets. Most new products that launch in the supermarkets don't last as long as SuperJam has and very few become as well loved.

I definitely didn't get everything right first time, and there were even points where I thought about giving up. I have certainly been on a very steep learning curve over the past few years. In this little book I'm not trying to preach to you or to pretend that I am some kind of business guru who knows the answers to everything. I am definitely not that.

Having said that, I have picked up a lot of useful advice along the way and learned all about the ups and downs of starting a company. There are a lot of things that I learned by making my mistakes. Hopefully by my sharing my story with you, these are the mistakes that you won't have to make too. If someone had given me this advice a few years ago, my business would have got to where it is today a lot more quickly and with many fewer sleepless nights.

I don't want to pretend that SuperJam's success has been entirely down to me; in fact, it has been almost entirely down to finding other people who believe in the idea as much as I do. In the early days, I was lucky enough to be supported by organisations like The Prince's Trust. As the business grew, I have learned from other entrepreneurs and even found a few to be my 'mentors'. They have built multimillion-pound companies and been willing to share the lessons they learned from it with me. I have scattered some of their inspirational stories, ideas and ways of doing things throughout this book, as well as some studies throughout on particular companies that have inspired me along the way.

By telling you about how SuperJam became a success, I want to give you an insight into how to come up with your own idea and get support from people who can help you make it happen. I want to help you prepare for the launch of your idea and understand how to listen to and love your customers. Hopefully I can also give you some advice about selling, generating publicity for your business, building a team and fostering a company culture, and about the importance of giving back to your community.

As well as sharing with you some of the things that I have picked up along the way, I'm also hoping to give you a sense of the excitement and thrill that I get from the whole enterprise. Nothing in my life has compared to the sense of achievement that I felt when I first saw my products on the supermarket shelf, for example.

It obviously takes a huge amount of hard work to get a business, new product or charity off the ground. You have to believe in your idea when everything seems to be going wrong and put everything you have into making it work. But, when it does work out in the end, it feels pretty amazing.

The SuperJam Story So Far

February 2005 – Invested £50 in hiring my first stall at a farmers' market, selling over 200 jars of jam, the most I had ever made!

August 2005 – Made the first delivery of my homemade jam to a shop, called The Store, in Stockbridge in Edinburgh.

September 2003 – Spent an afternoon learning my Gran's secret jam recipes!

Age 14   Age 15   Age 16   Age 17   Age 18   Age 19

February 2004 – Made the first batch of 'Doherty's Preserves', with labels I had designed on the computer, and sold the jars door to door for £1.50 each.

June 2006 – Channel 4 followed me around every day and supplied me with a mentor, John Boyle, as part of a documentary called *Tricky Business*.

March 2006 – Took my first few jars of SuperJam to a Waitrose 'Meet The Buyer' day, telling them all about my idea for making jam 100% from fruit.

March 2008 – The brand is launched on the shelves of the biggest retailer in the world, Wal-Mart, in its Asda stores in the UK, along with those of Morrisons. We celebrate reaching our thousandth outlet!

July 2008 – SuperJam is entered into an exhibition in the National Museum of Scotland as an example of an 'Iconic Scottish Brand', alongside Irn-Bru, Baxter's and Tunnock's Tea Cakes!

April 2007 – Made the first batch of SuperJam in the factory. It was something like 50,000 jars, more than I had made in the previous four years!

March 2007 – SuperJam launches in Waitrose, making me the youngest person ever to supply a major supermarket. We sold over 1,500 jars in one store on the first day!

November 2007 – Became the first ever person from outside North America to win the prestigious 'Global Student Entrepreneur of the Year Award'.

November 2007 – SuperJam launched nationally in Tesco, which became national news on the BBC, GMTV and *This Morning*, and I was even interviewed by the biggest news show in China!

Age 20   Age 21

March 2009
– Shared the front page of *The Sun* with worldwide singing sensation Susan Boyle, offering a free jar of SuperJam to all of *The Sun's* 5.5 million readers. My proudest moment of all!

August 2010 – *The SuperJam Cookbook* is launched, filled with recipes for how to make jam at home 100% from fruit and puddings that people can make with their homemade jam.

November 2010 – Became the first jam company in the world to launch an iPhone app, with recipes, videos and other fun bits and pieces.

December 2010 – Invited to start selling SuperJam, *The SuperJam Cookbook* and a range of SuperJam aprons and homewares on the home shopping channel QVC.

1 Why Start a Business?

How often do you get up on a Monday morning and feel excited about the week ahead, like you're doing what you love every day, what you were born to do?

There are a small number of people out there who spend every day doing what they've always dreamed of, doing what they feel in their gut is the right path for them. Maybe you're one of them, and I congratulate you if that's the case.

For one reason or another, a lot of people take the safe options in life or make the choices that they were told were right, and find themselves in jobs that unfortunately they don't love.

You've heard it a million times before and you'll hear it a million more, but happiness, enjoying every day and feeling fulfilled in yourself, is the most important thing in life. I find it really sad when I think of the millions of people who spend every day working in jobs that don't inspire them simply to pay the bills.

What makes me even sadder is that I know that everyone has what it takes to start a business or come up with a killer product or even set up a charity that could help thousands of people. The only thing stopping you is your mind, a fear of what might go wrong.

Maybe you fear the humiliation of failure, or quite reasonably are worried what might happen if you wind up not being able to keep up with your mortgage repayments. Perhaps you feel trapped in the daily cycle of work to pay the bills and look after your kids. It is fears and worries like these that stop you from giving your own venture a shot.

You may well feel that because of this, your family and friends might not be supportive of you taking the leap and leaving the security of what you're doing. You might be worried by the thought of having to quit your job and borrow a stack of money even to try your idea out. And then what happens if it doesn't work out and your business goes down the pan?

In my mind, these are fears that you don't have to feel. The risks you have to take to start your own business are a lot lower than you probably imagine. It is even possible to get an idea off the ground without the need to quit your job and without having to borrow a great deal of money.

It is super easy to try out your ideas in the evenings and weekends after work on a small scale without having to put huge amounts of money on the line. You don't have to jump in at the deep end and try to get your product into a thousand stores on day one. Think small. Make a few, see if people like them and take it from there. Once you have proven for sure that there is a market for your idea, *that's* when you can take the leap and leave your job or borrow money to take it to the next level.

It is commonly said that nine out of ten businesses fail. That simply isn't true; of course a lot of businesses are not as successful as their founder had hoped, but very few actually go bust.

I always suggest that, at whatever stage in life you're thinking of starting a business, you should make sure you have a safety net. Don't pack up your studies or your job right away, don't remortgage your house and don't spend your pension on your idea. If you don't take crazy risks, you'll be free to walk away at any point, if you feel it isn't working out like you had hoped.

I know it isn't easy to jump ship and change career. It's especially not easy when you have kids and mortgage payments to look after. That's why I'm fired up about encouraging young people not to start walking down a path in life that doesn't feel like them. It's a lot easier to follow your passion when you're young.

I'm really grateful that I was able to find my passion so early in life and could give it a shot without much risk. If my jam-making business hadn't taken off, it wouldn't have been such a big deal because I didn't have a family depending on me to make it work.

Although it is in some ways easier to follow your passion from day one, there is nothing stopping you making a change later in life, though. You might be having second thoughts in the middle of your career or even be retired. I've met loads of people who have left well-paid jobs in the City to start businesses, choosing to ditch the mad hours of the rat race for the flexibility that comes from setting up on your own.

Starting a small business can be whatever you want it to be; it can mean three days a week or seven, it can mean being out on the road selling or working from home. You can create a business to suit your lifestyle and grow it to whatever size you are comfortable with.

Family Influences

Where we find ourselves now in life has a huge amount to do with our families, where we grew up and the advice we received when we were younger.

Aside from perhaps my gran, there is nobody I need to thank more than my mum and dad for inspiring me to do what I love. When I was growing up they always let me make my own choices in life and never told me that I had to take a particular path.

When my dad was younger, his dream was to become a doctor. When he didn't get accepted to study medicine at Glasgow University, rather than staying at school to get the grades he needed, he decided to become an engineer. At the time, electrical engineering was being heavily promoted as the future for Scotland.

I was still growing up when my dad was made redundant and I saw the problems he and his friends had with the fear of job loss due to the nature of the technical industries in Scotland. By the time I was in my teens, he had taken a break from being an engineer to become a lecturer. Although he was a great teacher, he found working in colleges frustrating and ended up not particularly enjoying his work.

Of course, had he ignored what everyone said and become a doctor, he would have been a lot more successful and found himself enjoying his work a lot more.

Having seen my dad do what 'they' told him taught me to listen only to my heart and to put all of my energy into doing what I love. That means I didn't listen too carefully to the advice of careers advisers or anyone who laughed at my jam idea. After my dad was made redundant, I didn't have a lot of faith in the security of salaried jobs.

When I was a kid, I was always coming up with harebrained ideas to try to make some extra pocket money. A lot of parents wouldn't let their kids try things out like mine did, but I think they wanted me to make mistakes and learn from them. Thankfully, they never tried to force me to become a doctor or a lawyer or anything else that I didn't want to be. They knew the importance of doing what makes you happy.

Being Your Own Boss

My first few attempts at setting up my own little business weren't really much of a success, as you'll find out later. It was fun each time, though, and I soon began to decide that one day I would start a real business and it would be my career. I concluded that I never wanted to work for anyone other than myself and at 14 started to really think about how I was going to set up my first proper business.

When you make that decision to start up your own business, you are setting yourself a challenge and putting faith in your own ability to make it happen. You have an idea that you believe in so much that you nurture it over years and years until you get to where you're trying to go.

Having the idea is the first step. Then you have to figure out how to make it happen and convince yourself to work hard enough to get things moving. There isn't anyone there telling you to do the work in the morning—you have to tell yourself.

When you're employed, you rely on your boss to value you, respect you and take care of you. In many companies, as an employee, you're little more than a number. The bosses' motivation in the morning is not to make your life better; it is to enrich themselves and their shareholders. If they can do that by laying you off, they will.

So setting up on your own is about taking the responsibility for creating your employment fully into your own hands, not relying on a big company or the government to keep you in a job. It's down to you, which can sometimes mean a lot of pressure and sleepless nights. But it also means a great deal of satisfaction from knowing that all of the fruits of your labour are yours to keep. After tax, at least!

And even though you may have to work on your idea in the evenings and weekends after work, when you're already exhausted, it shouldn't really feel like work. When you're doing what feels right in your gut, the excitement and adrenaline of seeing your ideas becoming reality motivates you to work harder than you've ever worked before. If what you're doing is authentic to who you are, it comes easily.

What is important is having that desire to give things a go and wanting to do them purely for the thrill and fun of it. There are continual setbacks in setting up a business and a lot of ideas fail completely. But if things don't work out in the way you had hoped, you can always learn something from the experience. The most important skill is having a willingness to try again, try something new or change your idea a little, based on what you learned from its not working out. As an entrepreneur, you get satisfaction from trying again and again until one of your ideas is eventually successful. And, when it is, you'll have the pleasure of getting up in the morning and being in charge of your day, and of being your own boss.

Being an Entrepreneur

Being an entrepreneur is a whole way of life. It isn't necessarily about being a 'businessman', wearing a suit or sitting in an office working on a computer; it can be whatever you want it to be. It's up to you what you wear, what hours you work and which ideas you try out. You can choose to spend every waking hour on your business or take time out for the things you value in life: your family, friends, interests and community. It's about looking at life as a big adventure and feeling like you can give anything a shot. You have that big idea and you don't stop thinking about it from the moment you wake up until the moment you go to sleep.

Entrepreneurs are a bunch of people who look at the world differently to everyone else, see things we don't like and try to change them. We have a certain spark that drives us to look for opportunities and to try to solve problems in the world around us.

Entrepreneurs are everywhere. Think of all the people who create new products, set up small companies, social enterprises and charities. Maybe you're a Dyson who wants to build a better vacuum cleaner or an Anita Roddick who's horrified by the idea of testing cosmetics on animals.

I started my entrepreneurial journey very young, although some people start even younger than I did. In a lot of ways, starting at such a young age has an advantage: the naivety of youth makes any dream seem possible!

When I was about 10, I visited a chicken farm and was fascinated by the business of collecting eggs from the hens. I asked the farmer if I could have a box of eggs, so that I could hatch them into chickens of my own, and sell their eggs.

The farmer gave me half a dozen eggs and laughed, saying that there was no way I could hatch them into chickens. She joked that I'd have to sit on them for three weeks.

When I told my parents about my idea, they weren't too pleased at the prospect of having chickens running around, as you can imagine, but they said that I could give it a go. I suppose they doubted that I would manage to hatch out the eggs.

I then had to figure out how I was going to keep a box of eggs warm around the clock for about three weeks. I thought about using lots of hot water bottles, putting the eggs in the oven on a really low temperature or maybe leaving them in a greenhouse. Obviously, none of these ideas was going to work. Eventually, I had the idea of keeping the eggs on top of the cable TV box under the television. It was quite warm there if the telly was left on all the time.

I waited anxiously for weeks, checking every day that the eggs were OK. Finally, one morning, everyone was sitting eating breakfast and we could hear a little chirping coming from under the television. The first fluffy yellow chick had hatched out of its egg. I named her Henrietta, which, being 10 years old, I believed to be quite a witty name for a hen. Later in the day, another two of the chicks hatched and so I had to start thinking about what I was actually going to do with them.

Once the chicks got a bit bigger, my dad built a little house in the garden for them to live in. They soon started to lay delicious fresh eggs every day, which the neighbours were more than happy to buy from me for £1 a box. I had a lot of fun doing this, until a fox came and ate all of the chickens, rather tragically putting an end to my farming career. I was completely devastated.

Although this wasn't really much of a business, it was my first taste of being an entrepreneur. I got a buzz from that early little project and started thinking of more and more ideas as time went on. I always felt that this was the way that I could have an impact on the world.

Of course, you don't have to be young to start a business and I am amazed and inspired by the companies that are started by people who have caught the bug later in life. They have the advantage of experience, of life and of the commercial world, when they come to start their companies.

The reason I'm sharing my story with you is not because I think it'll make you a millionaire. Starting your own business just might do that, but I hope that you'll be more excited by the prospect of going on an amazing adventure, having a lot of fun and, if it all works, bringing about a change in the world around you.

What Do You Want from Life?

The absolutely most important question to ask yourself before you embark on anything in life is: Why? Why am I starting a business?

There are all kinds of motivations for starting a business. Some people want job security while others simply dream of becoming rich. More often than not, people believe that they will feel they are doing something more worthwhile, more fulfilling and more exciting with their life than whatever it is they're doing currently. Wouldn't you rather be doing something that made you happier and was more fun, even if it was for less money than you get from what you're doing now?

Of course, for me and for more and more start-ups, the underlying motivation is a desire to have an impact on the world in a positive way. It isn't about trying to fulfil the dream of one day being able to cruise around the Bahamas, gallivanting about with beautiful people, as wonderful as I'm sure that would be! It is about taking satisfaction from solving a problem in the world, doing something worthwhile in life and, of course, hopefully making a living from doing it.

There are lots of inspirational companies who have really embraced this and have much more of a sense of purpose than only making profit. Think of Innocent, The Body Shop, Ben and Jerry's, Patagonia, One Water and even Jamie Oliver.

Often, I find that my generation of entrepreneurs are willing to invest a lot of their time and profits in doing good for a particular community. Getting rich isn't the most important motivation in their lives. In my case, I take far more satisfaction from an elderly person telling me that our tea parties make them feel like a person again than I could ever take from trying to make lots of money to buy expensive clothes, for example.

Your motivation for getting into business is something personal to you and will determine what your goals and expectations are. It's up to you to decide how ambitious you want to be, how big you dream of your company becoming, or how important it is that you get to take time out for holidays, for your family and for fun.

In this book, I really want to give you the sense that a tiny idea that can start in a kitchen or a bedroom or a garden shed, with a bit of love and hard work and support from the people around you, could grow into something amazing. Something that gives you a career, and maybe even creates a priceless opportunity to support your community. Something that changes your life—I know that SuperJam has changed mine.

2 Eureka! Super Idea

Have you found your super idea yet? You might have a hunch about the kind of business you'd like to start, but it doesn't matter too much if you don't. I'm going to give you some insight into how you can come up with some great ideas.

There are all sorts of places you can look to find your killer idea. You might use a skill that you've already taken the time to learn or maybe there's a problem you have come across in your day-to-day life that you reckon you could solve. Perhaps you'll be one of the people who will be able to figure out how to evolve your hobby into a career, so you can make a living from something you love.

Wherever you choose to look for your idea, there are a few factors that will lead to success or failure. The most important question to ask yourself is whether you will be offering something worthwhile, something that people will be willing to pay their hard-earned money for.

Of course, you need to create something that is different to what is already out there and that will capture the imagination of your customers. It doesn't have to be something radically different; maybe you'll offer great customer service in a sector where nobody else does (think of First Direct or Egg in banking), or maybe you'll present something that has been around for ages but in a funky new way. Whatever you do, it has to be something that excites you to your core and that feels authentic to who you are and what you believe in.

It is also important to think about whether or not you will enjoy making that product or providing that service. To get the business started, you're going to have to spend a lot of time on it and you probably won't make much money at the start. It has to be something that you're going to find fun, challenging and exciting to do, regardless of the amount of work involved or how little money you might make.

Coming up with that idea doesn't have to be difficult and the best ideas in the world are usually very simple. You really don't need to reinvent the wheel. I know I certainly haven't.

Finding Inspiration

My idea came about very simply from my love of my gran's jam. I took inspiration from her and ran with it. Your gran might not be as good at cooking as mine, so perhaps you will have to look more widely for inspiration to start your business.

People tell me all the time that they want to start a business but they can't think of an idea. Maybe that's a frustration that you feel too. I always ask them: how much time have you spent trying to come up with an idea? Almost always, their answer is 'none'. It's as if people have an impression that ideas just pop into your head one day as if by magic, like they do in cartoons.

How many ideas have you had lying in the bath or on a beach? Probably loads and loads. When you take time out from the chaos of day-to-day life to stop and think, even for just a moment, that is when you start to have ideas.

If you were to devote even just a day to coming up with ideas, you would be amazed at what you can come up with when your entire mind is focused on it. Think about the following and try to see the business opportunities in each:

♦ How could you make day-to-day life better for disabled people?

♦ How could you encourage people to holiday in East Sussex?

♦ What would make it simpler for people to grow potatoes at home?

♦ Is there a service you could create to prevent people running out of toilet paper?

♦ Could you create a system that makes it easier for employees to claim expenses from their employer and for the employer to pay them?

♦ How could you make a living out of a passion for tulips?

See how simple it can be? It's not for me to tell you what topics are interesting to you or not, but I can guarantee that there are almost limitless opportunities for each. I don't think you're going to start an internet television show about tulip growing, but someone will!

How to Come Up with a Super Idea

- ◆ Take time out
- ◆ Pick a theme that interests you (e.g. Wales, joinery, computer games)
- ◆ Find as many problems to do with that theme as you can
- ◆ Take note of everything annoying in your daily life
- ◆ Be interested in everything; inspiration can come from anywhere
- ◆ Research your market and ask questions
- ◆ Look at boring industries, dominated by a few big old companies
- ◆ Learn about and visit companies that inspire you
- ◆ Find out about what's taking off in other countries
- ◆ Check out sites like springwise.com to find out about new business ideas

You'll no doubt be able to come up with hundreds of ideas, some of them awful and some of them good, for whatever topics or themes that interest you. In a way, you have to open yourself up to looking at everything with a critical eye. Try to find flaws in products and services you use every day and come up with ways to make them better.

Do you forget to send birthday cards to loved ones? Or maybe you get annoyed when the milk goes off in your fridge? Or you spend hours flicking through channels trying to find something you want to watch? Does the amount of junk in kids' food make you angry? How about the rubbish they serve as meals in hospitals?

If it's not you, someone will solve all of those problems sooner or later. When you get into it, you discover that there are hundreds, if not thousands, of things that annoy you that you could change.

One of the big barriers that people often put up in their minds is: 'If it's a good idea, surely it's already been done.' There is some truth in that, but in reality, if you look at products you use every day, you can soon get into the mindset that almost everything in the world is badly designed or not good value for money and very few companies offer decent customer service.

Look around you at everything in your daily life. How many of the things you buy inspire you? How many things do you buy and think 'Wow, this is the best pair of shoes I've ever bought', or 'This is incredible value for money', or 'What great customer service I just had'?

Once you come round to the way of thinking that everything can and should be improved, you realize that the possibilities for new products are limited only by your imagination.

You might be afraid of trying to come up with ideas because you don't consider yourself to be a 'creative person'. I don't believe in the notion that some people are creative and some people aren't. How many kids like drawing or making things or coming up with imaginative stories? All of them. So you did too! But somewhere along the way, most people get an idea in their heads that they aren't creative, that coming up with ideas isn't for them.

I am often invited to speak in schools and sometimes we set the kids a challenge of coming with their own ideas for inventions. Within 30 minutes, we have a roomful of kids with literally hundreds of ideas for new products. Some of them are pretty wacky, but every now and then they come up with something that might just work.

If you were to be more like a kid and simply take the attitude that no idea is too crazy, that anything is possible, you'd find yourself coming up with ideas all the time.

Be Interested in Everything

I've already mentioned why I think it is important that you spend your time working on ideas that interest and inspire you. Of course, there are some things that will interest you more than anything else and those that are personal to you; for all I care you might find accountancy, termites, databases or cheese interesting and want to come up with an idea that lets you spend all your time working on that.

Having said that, you should always make an effort to take an interest in everything. Go out of your way to learn about topics that you don't know anything about, talk to people you wouldn't normally talk to and go to places you've never thought of going to before.

Ask questions all the time, be curious about where things come from, how much they cost, how they are made. Read women's magazines, *The Economist*, the *Daily Mail*, *New Scientist*, children's books, everything. Watch trashy television, home shopping channels, even documentaries about moles—open yourself up to experiences and viewpoints that you would normally shut yourself off from.

Why on earth would you want to do all this?

Everything in the world is connected to everything else. Ideas don't come to you in isolation; great ones arrive where you take inspiration from one place and join it up with something you have learned in another.

When you are a child you learn the fastest, come up with the most ideas and have the most fun. Kids ask questions all the time and it is all because they are interested in everything.

Gaps in the Market

Once you have a topic that interests you or maybe a hunch about an idea, you need to learn everything you can about the topic. Become an expert. Read the annual reports and press releases of companies in the field to find out what they are talking about. Find out all about the market by getting your hands on market research reports from companies like Mintel and Datamonitor. They will tell you who your competitors are, which products are the best sellers in the category and what kinds of people are buying them.

It goes without saying that you should ask everyone you can what they think about the topic. If you're trying to come up with a product for people who fish, go to fishing conventions. Get into the mind of the people who you will one day be selling to. Why do they like going fishing? What are the problems they come up against? What tools in their kit do they use the most often?

Soon, you'll get a sense of where the market is heading—what the next big things are in fishing, for instance. You might discover that the market is in decline and very few people are being attracted to it, or maybe it's growing like crazy and people are building successful businesses without even having the best products on the market.

A good way of finding ideas is to look at markets that are dominated by a few big players, who have been around for a long time and haven't innovated much. The jam industry was such a place, where big family companies had being doing the same old thing for generations.

There are all sorts of products that have barely changed in 100 years. Often, without an entrepreneur like you coming into a market like that, innovation would never happen. It can take someone from outside the industry to see what needs to change.

All of the products we buy today were, at one time, state of the art, in fashion or something that people were excited by. Now, because they haven't changed with the times or been improved over the years, there are all sorts of products that we don't love any more. You can find a way of repackaging, redesigning or remarketing them to appeal to the modern consumer.

When you find yourself looking at a market that has been in decline for a long time, ask why. Perhaps people don't buy that product any longer because it is too unhealthy, too expensive, or takes too long to reach them. In a market like that, you have to find a new way of creating or delivering that product, solving the problems you have spotted.

You might be attracted to a market that is growing like crazy. In markets that are growing fast, the companies in them are not well established and so there is an opportunity to disrupt the market by launching something cheaper, faster, healthier or with better features. In this case, you need to be willing to hit the ground running and continually improve and add to your idea, because in a market like that you could be left behind in the blink of an eye. This is especially true in the high-tech world. Think of everything that has been outdated almost as quickly as it became fashionable: MiniDisk players, for instance, were quickly replaced by MP3 players, which were soon blown out of the water by the iPod.

Being Inspired by Other Companies

Almost every day, I come across a new product in the supermarket, online or in a magazine that inspires me. None of them has anything to do with jam, but I have taken ideas and ways of thinking from all of them. I've visited lots of the companies, met their founders and tried to understand what makes companies like Innocent, Feel Good Drinks, Method, Graze, Eat Natural, Walker's Shortbread and dozens of others so special.

There is nothing to stop you from writing to companies that inspire you and asking if you can visit them or even interview the founders. Companies like Innocent even suggest on their packaging that you should visit them in person to find out more about what they do. You could seek out paid or unpaid work for a company you admire, to try to understand how their business works so well.

You can find a company that has reinvented a product, figure out how it was done, and then do the same thing for the kind of product that interests you.

Finding Ideas from Other Countries

I love travelling and visiting places that are off the beaten track, finding quirky little ideas and ways of doing things that are unique to a particular place. Drinking the local tipple, tasting the specialities of that area and finding out what people do for fun.

There are endless lists of products that are popular in some countries but haven't reached others yet. People go on holiday to a country and come home having developed a taste for a particular drink or style of music or design of clothes. What's stopping you from finding an idea that is successful in another country and bringing it to your own?

A lot of the time, it is a sure sign that if something is taking off in America, it will soon travel around the world and make it big in most western countries. Think about smoothies and cupcakes, for instance. Sahar Hashemi saw the coffeehouse phenomenon taking off in the US and, when she came back to the UK, started Coffee Republic with her brother and became a huge success from it. What are the things that are taking off in the US or elsewhere in the world now that you think might one day be popular in your country too?

Road Test It

The best way to figure out whether your idea is any good is to ask everyone you can what they think. I come across far too many people who are frightened of telling anyone their ideas, worried that someone might 'steal' them.

If you're one of those people, take a moment to ask yourself whether the idea you have is really so simple that anyone could copy it. If it is, maybe you need to work on it a bit so that it is more exciting and individual. Chances are, it is your enthusiasm for it that makes it a good idea and the way you will protect it is by building a great brand around it.

Don't be afraid of telling people your ideas. Share them with the world and, who knows, someone might just be able to help you make them happen.

Get your friends and family involved and, most importantly, involve your potential customers in the adventure that is your start-up business.

Keep It Super Simple

Once you have researched your market extensively and taken on board all of the feedback of your family, friends and potential customers, you can hopefully refine your idea down until it is super simple to explain. You should be so clear in your mind about what makes your idea a winner that you can explain it in one or two sentences. That's what is sometimes referred to as an 'elevator pitch', where you can explain to someone really simply why they should support, invest in or buy your idea. If you're not able to explain it in a simple way, you probably aren't clear enough in your own mind about what it is you want to do. And how do you expect anyone else to be clear about your idea if you're not?

The most foolproof test to find out if you have refined your idea enough is to try explaining it to your gran. You should be able to tell her all about it in a language that is free from jargon and with a clear reason for why anyone would spend their money on it.

Sam Walton might have explained his Wal-Mart idea as 'a general store that attracts people through its doors by having the lowest prices in town, which means we can buy in bulk, cut costs and offer even lower prices'. Anita Roddick might have described her Body Shop idea as 'a cosmetics shop that doesn't test its products on animals and campaigns for issues important to us'. Even the biggest ideas in the history of business can be summed up in a sentence.

You need to have some idea of how your product or service is going to be put together. How easy is it going to be to get things up and running, what is your product or service going to cost to produce or provide, and how you will be able to offer it at a price that people will be willing to pay?

You have to be certain that your creation is going to have a wide enough market for you to be able to make a real business out of it. It doesn't have to be a blockbuster, multimillion-unit-selling idea, but you must be sure that there are enough people out there who are longing for your product to make it a viable company.

What Is a Good Idea?

Great ideas solve some kind of problem that lots of people relate to and they usually do it in a really simple way. Of course, there's a difference between a great idea and a great business.

Some of my friends in Germany, Phil, Hubertus and Max, discovered that everyone likes different things in their muesli. So they came up with Mymuesli.com, a site where people can come up with their own combination of fruits, nuts, chocolates and other ingredients to make muesli that is individual to them. It's a really simple concept that has taken off in Germany and elsewhere in Europe, with sales exceeding a million euros.

What makes Mymuesli a great idea is that it has mass-market appeal, it's easy to explain and is something that people find really engaging. It is a lot of fun being able to come up with a breakfast cereal that is completely your own creation. The business also has pretty good margins and was relatively easy to start off small and scale up over time.

You have to ask whether there is a big enough market for your idea for you to make any real money from it, and long-term money at that. Is yours an idea that can stand the test of time, that won't be obliterated by some small change in the law or the market or people's tastes? Hopefully you can imagine that people will come back again and again to buy your product and will become loyal to your brand.

Be aware that family and friends can say what they think is the right thing, that your idea is fantastic, when sometimes it might need a bit of work. The only way to know for sure is to give it a shot.

You will no doubt have had moments when you see a new product on the market and you say 'Why didn't I think of that?' or 'Why hadn't anyone done that before?'—that's the sign of a good idea. Someone has put thought into creating something and it fits perfectly into the world, it makes perfect sense.

My 'Eureka' Moment

When I was about 13, I got a job for a local entrepreneur selling bacon and sausages door to door. It wasn't really a normal job for a teenager, but I thought it was a lot of fun at the time. I had a list of regular customers, whom I visited every week, to deliver them fresh bacon. Over a year or so I had built up a great relationship with them and I was soon selling a lot of bacon every week.

My sales were more than any of the other teenagers who were doing the same job and the boss was very impressed. After a while, he gave me a job training other young people how to sell bacon door to door and he taught me all about how he ran his business.

He was probably the first entrepreneur I had come across and I found his way of life fascinating. Seeing him growing his business and being in control of his lifestyle made me more and more certain that I wanted to start up a business of my own one day.

Around this time, I was visiting my gran and she happened to be cooking a pot of jam when we arrived, in the same way as she had for as long as I could remember. She knew everything about making the best jam and had perfected her recipes over decades. Everyone, especially me, has always loved my gran's jam and she was often cooking it up for family and friends when we visited.

This was when I had my eureka moment. I realized that I could start my own business making jam, using my gran's well-loved secret recipes. I decided that I would sell the jam door to door, just as I had done with bacon and sausages for the past year or so. It was a very simple plan and I could barely contain my excitement—I was finally going to create my own business!

Delivering an Old Product in a New Way: Graze (graze.com)

The innovation for your business idea might not involve completely reinventing a product, but rather finding a novel way for people to buy and receive it.

Graze is one of my favourite start-up companies. Begun by a friend of mine called Graham Bosher, who also set up the phenomenally successful LoveFilm, along with his friends, it is a really simple concept: fresh fruit, nuts and healthy snacks delivered to your home or office on a daily subscription.

There are all kinds of products that I use in my day-to-day life that I'd love to set up a subscription for, so that I don't need to worry about remembering to buy them every time they run out. There is a company in Belgium called Raz*War that has applied the subscription model to razor blades. Wine clubs, book clubs and even chocolate clubs all prosper by having a subscription-based business model. Customers tend to be really loyal when you make it easy to set up a weekly, monthly or yearly payment to receive your products.

I visited the 'Graze Kitchen', where the magic happens, when they first started out and found it a really inspirational business. When you sign up, you can select which of the snacks you think you'll love and which ones you don't fancy as much. They'll send you a different box every day, every other day, or just once a week if you prefer. The boxes are beautifully designed and the whole service offers a really simple solution to the problem of not getting your 'five a day'. There is nothing new or very exciting about selling people fresh fruit, nuts and snacks, but Graze managed to come up with a whole new model for delivering them.

3 Finding Support

I convinced my gran to teach me her jam-making secrets and give me all of the advice that I needed to start making it myself. We spent an afternoon making jam together, which I found fascinating, and I got super excited about the prospect of starting my own little jam business.

When we got home, I ran round to the supermarket and invested about £2 in a few oranges and a bag of sugar. I made the first few jars of marmalade that afternoon and took them round the street in a plastic bucket. I couldn't even wait for the jars to cool down properly before visiting the neighbours, I was too excited.

I returned home having sold those first few jars with about £4 in my pocket. I felt like I had accomplished something huge: I had created a profit completely on my own, with nothing more than a few oranges and some sugar. I waited anxiously for a week, before returning to those first few customers to hear their verdicts on my jam.

All of them had loved the jam and immediately bought more; some even bought extra jars for their friends. Their support encouraged me to start visiting more houses and to come up with some new recipes.

I was all fired up about my little business and couldn't wait to start knocking on doors to build up a list of regular customers to deliver to.

I designed some labels on the computer and started calling the business 'Doherty's Preserves'. I printed off some leaflets that I could give to people, explaining the story behind the business and also how high quality the products were. My homemade preserves were all natural and made with top-quality local fruit. I wanted to make sure that my customers and potential customers knew why the products were so great.

Slowly Building Up

Within a couple of months I was visiting about 50 houses every month and had a range of three products, two jams and one marmalade. I was making about £20 a week at this point, for tens of hours of work. That didn't matter, though; I knew that I would soon be able to invest in bigger pans and would be able to make much more jam in the evenings after school.

I soon had a few of my friends helping with the deliveries and was making hundreds of jars of jam every month. The business wasn't really making much profit, but I had a good feeling about the future and it was a huge amount of fun.

I began getting invited to local events, like church fêtes and gala days, where I set up a stall to sell my increasingly popular products. My school even let me set up a stall at the Christmas concert and at parents' evenings. All of this helped to build a brand locally and people started talking about 'the jam boy'. Word was spreading about my business and local people were supporting me in whatever ways they could.

There is no doubt that the first place you should look for support is your friends, family and your local community.

They are more likely to be open and honest with you about what they think are the pitfalls of your idea and I'm sure they'll be happy to support you in whatever way they can.

My family and friends were usually my guinea pigs for deciding whether or not a new recipe was good enough to be added to the range. Some recipes didn't make it past this stage, like banana jam, which just didn't look very nice!

Having been going for about a year, the business was growing nicely and I had started generating strong sales every week. I was also managing to keep up with the production, since I had invested in two large pans and was getting help with labelling and deliveries from my friends and my younger brother, Connor.

I had to work very hard to keep all of this under control in the weekends and after school. Once we were making deliveries all over the local area, it became hard to figure out how to grow the business. I was also struggling to make a profit from all of this hard work, especially by the time I had paid my friends something for their time. Pretty soon, I needed to come up with an idea for taking the business on to the next level, an idea that was shortly to arrive.

Taking the Leap

Encouraged by all of the support that people were giving me for my fledgling business, I decided to leave school to focus all of my energies on trying to turn what was really just a jam-making hobby into my career. I was little more than 16 years old at this point and, as you can imagine, making the decision to go into the 'real world' seemed quite daunting.

Starting a business can be a lonely experience. It is usually something that you work on alone, or maybe with a business partner. It's your project in the garden shed, your obsession that nobody else around you quite gets.

A big question is always who you can turn to for help. If, like me, your family doesn't run its own business and none of your friends do, it can sometimes feel like you're the only entrepreneur around.

For me, being so young when I started out, I wasn't very sure where to turn to for advice. Although my family and friends were all very excited to see me setting up a business and supported me in whatever way they could, getting an idea off the ground wasn't something any of them had experience of.

Finding a Mentor

I've been amazed by the number of people willing to give advice to young people starting out in business. I benefited from the help of a successful local entrepreneur called Kevin Dorren, who had already built a dot-com company and floated it on the stock market. Having set up a successful business himself, supplying low-carbohydrate snack bars to big supermarkets, Kevin got in touch after reading about my story in the local newspaper.

He said that he loved to see young people with ideas for their own companies and that my story reminded himself of when he was young, trying to set up a small business. He explained that a lot of people had given him advice over the years that helped him get his ideas off the ground, and so he was more than happy to share the lessons that he had learned along the way with someone else starting out on the same path.

Kevin agreed to meet with me every few months and he taught me all about his business, explained how supermarkets worked and shared stories about where things hadn't gone so well for him.

He also put me in touch with some of his contacts, such as suppliers and even potential customers along the way, and proved to be a great sounding board for my sometimes mad ideas.

I was also lucky enough to be put in touch with an ex-Tesco buyer called Tony, who had left the world of large corporates to set up his own company. He had registered with a government scheme that connected businesspeople with young entrepreneurs who needed a mentor.

Everyone starting out in business should try to find someone like Kevin or Tony. There are government programmes to link entrepreneurs with a mentor and also charities like The Prince's Trust that can help you find one. But I would say that the best thing to do is to find a success story that really inspires you, or an entrepreneur whom you very much admire. Find your hero. Get in touch with them, tell them your story and explain your dream; ask if you can meet them at their office for 20 minutes to ask a bit of advice.

When you meet them, you absolutely must respect their time; they are helping you out of the goodness of their heart. They are giving up their time to give you advice because they enjoy helping other entrepreneurs to get their ideas off the ground. Make sure that you have useful, to-the-point questions that can really make the most of your meeting with them. Ask how they did it, what they would do in your situation, who you should be speaking to, what you should be reading and so on.

You're looking for someone who has been there and done it before and who can point out the pitfalls, share stories of their mistakes and make connections to people who might be able to turn your ideas into reality.

Experienced businesspeople are willing to spend their time giving advice in this way because it offers them the opportunity to learn about a whole new business than their own. You have to bear in mind that it is down to you to respect the relationship and not ask too much of your mentors. You should only really ask them major questions about the direction of your business, not day-to-day things that you could easily work out yourself. If you get on well with your mentor and they learn something from the experience, they will no doubt be willing to give you a lot of their time and really help to make your ideas happen.

Creating a Board

If you want to find someone who can devote more time to helping to come up with ideas for your business and solve problems that you are facing, you might want to consider putting together a board. This is where you employ a few experienced people to give you advice on the direction you should take the business in. They won't work in the company day to day, but will be able to give you advice on what direction you should take the business in, based on their experiences. They will have a totally different perspective of your business than you do, which means they will come up with different opinions and ideas for what you should do next.

Your board might only consist of one or two other people whom you can meet with as often as you feel is appropriate; something between four and eight times a year would be fairly standard for a start-up business.

Finding people to invite onto your board is a lot like finding a mentor. You are looking for someone who has different experiences than your own, who has perhaps had success in a similar kind of business and ideally who has contacts you can take advantage of to grow your company.

How you attract these people to sit on your board is down to you, but you can consider offering them a small stake in your company in exchange for their expertise; they will be motivated most to help you succeed if you do.

Alternatively, you can simply pay them a fee for their time, making them a non-executive director, a role that I hold in a number of fast-growing food and drink companies. Their name being connected to the company alone, if they are well known, can be worth its weight in gold. In essence, a non-executive director is someone whom you employ to provide advice on the direction of the business, by meeting up with you for board meetings throughout the year.

Raising Finance

Going from the eureka moment of SuperJam to actually seeing the finished product on the shelves was a process that required hundreds of thousands of pounds of investment. Since I wasn't in a position to raise any finance from a bank or investor, being so young, I had to figure out how to get my ideas off the ground without much financial backing at all.

My family certainly wasn't in a position to lend me any money and I had little more than a few thousand pounds in savings, mostly money that I had made from selling homemade jam on a relatively small scale for the previous year or two.

Money was needed for product development, design, jars, lids, fruit and promoting the story to the press. All of those things cost money that I simply didn't have, so I had to consider all of the different options available to me for raising finance. I spoke to charities, such as The Prince's Trust, and even met with potential investors and banks, sharing my business plan with them.

Grants and Soft Loans

I needed some money to pay for the first supermarket promotions, printing leaflets, travelling to meetings with supermarket buyers and other bits and pieces.

I applied to the Prince's Trust (the Prince's Scottish Youth Business Trust in Scotland) for a £5,000 loan and also for a £1,000 grant.

It's a wonderful charity, backed by Prince Charles, supporting hundreds if not thousands of young people to get set up in business. It provides loans, grants and advice to anyone with a bright idea who is struggling to raise money in the mainstream way.

I was one such person and the charity loved my idea. It agreed to issue the loan and grant and, as it does with every loan, agreed not to break my legs if things didn't work out and I ended up not being able to pay it back.

There are all kinds of places to look for grants, which is money that you don't have to pay back, and I have listed some of them at the back of this book. The government often offers grants to people who are starting up, especially if you are investing in research and development or are likely to create lots of jobs.

There's also a huge amount of support for businesses that plan on exporting to other countries. In the case of SuperJam, we were invited to exhibit our products at a trade fair in

Dubai. This helped us to get our products stocked by some distributors and retailers over there. The government contributed towards the cost of flights and paid for our stand at the event, which was fantastic support and made it possible for SuperJam to promote its products in a market that we otherwise wouldn't have been able to reach.

Borrowing from the Bank

If you aren't eligible for a grant or a soft loan from the government or someone like The Prince's Trust, you might have to consider borrowing money from the bank.

I don't want to recommend that anyone risk their house and pension on their idea; there is always another way that doesn't involve taking crazy risks that could wind up ruining your life. I have seen many entrepreneurs learn these risks the hard way. In most cases, you should do whatever you can to avoid signing a personal guarantee for the debt of your business.

If you have to borrow money, check out the Enterprise Finance Guarantee, which allows you to borrow the money to start your business from a high-street bank without risking your house. Instead, for a modest fee, the government will become the guarantor on your loan; which means that if your idea doesn't work out, the government will pay back your loan. That way, the bank can't hound you personally to get its money back.

There could be all sorts of other options available to you, other than just taking out a loan from the bank. Depending on what you need the money for, the bank may be able to help you out in a way that doesn't place any risk on your shoulders.

For instance, you might need to borrow money for working capital, things like stock and providing credit to your customers. In this case, it might make sense for you to 'factor' your debtors, which is where the bank pays you up front for money that you know is coming in further down the line; taking a fee along the way, of course. That way, you won't have to worry about collecting money from your customers and by getting their money in the door quicker, you might not need to borrow as much from the bank.

Finding an Investor

You will no doubt already have given some thought to the option of finding an investor for your idea; perhaps inspired by BBC's *Dragon's Den*. Although I didn't choose this route, it makes a lot of sense for many entrepreneurs.

Finding someone to invest in your idea could mean taking on a partner who has the cash to back you and also wants to work in the business with you. Or it might mean finding an 'angel investor', who specializes in putting up the money to get ideas off the ground, to buy a stake in the business.

Who you choose to bring into your business, whether day to day or merely as an outside investor, will be one of the biggest decisions you make. You need to be cautious not to share too much control of your business with someone else, unless you're totally sure it's the best thing to do.

I would personally be fearful that if I took on outside investment and they didn't understand why I do things the way I do, they might not support things like our charity work or let me try out crazy ideas every once and again.

However, as long as your investor understands your vision for where you're trying to go and can make a worthwhile contribution to help you get there, by supplying you with contacts, advice or ideas, it can be a beautiful relationship.

Getting Your Customers to Back You

Something I'm really fascinated by is the phenomenon of entrepreneurs asking consumers to back their idea from the offset. This involves getting the individuals who love their idea to buy a share in it, or even pre-order the product before it has been made. This can raise all of the money needed to get prototypes created, or set up premises or produce the first batch.

This idea has really taken off in the music industry with sites like slicethepie.com, where music fans can buy a 'share' in an up-and-coming musician. The artist can use the money to record their album and, once it's launched, shares the profits with their fans. A site called kickstarter.com expands the concept to include filmmakers, performers, designers and all sorts of other creative types. What's wonderful about the internet is that no matter how crazy your idea for a film or how niche your comic book concept, there are thousands of people out there somewhere who would love to see it happen. There are all kinds of ideas that banks or conventional investors wouldn't touch but that fans are more than happy to back.

Although this is a really unconventional way to raise money, I really love it and think it's a model I would consider if SuperJam ever needs to raise money in the future. I can't think of anyone better to have as a shareholder than someone who really loves the brand and wants to see it succeed in the long term. I'd go as far as to say that the kind of people who would invest in a band they love or a brand they love are the kind of people who would tell all their friends about it, send in their ideas and do everything they could to help make it a success.

The real value in getting your customer to back your idea is that you can get instant feedback from the very people who are going to be buying your product. By involving as many people as possible in the process of developing your business, you will gain access to a far wider range of ideas and opinions than you would have on your own.

If potential customers feel that they have been involved in developing your product and business, there's no doubt that they will be very loyal to it. If you've taken on board their contribution and made what they think is a great product, they're certainly going to buy it from you when it launches. They might even proudly tell their friends about your product or service, and how they helped you get started, once it gets off the ground.

Your potential customers' feedback on your concept is gold dust. If all of your customers tell that you should bring it out in red or with chocolate chips or that you should offer free delivery, that's exactly what you should do. If you can involve them in the process of developing your product, you're on to a winner.

Getting support for your idea from your customers: BrewDog (brewdog.com)

Scotland's largest independent brewery, BrewDog is a really fun and inspirational company. Set up by two of my friends, James Watt and Martin Dickie, it makes a range of quality ales, stouts and beers with really fun branding. It flies in the face of the conventional brands that dominate the category with names like Anchor, Steam Boat and Badger, offering instead Punk IPA, Tokyo and Sink the Bismarck.

James and Martin produce hilarious and edgy videos that are watched by hundreds of thousands of people on YouTube. They have courted controversy by producing the strongest (and most expensive) beer in the world, The End of History (55% alcohol and £500 a bottle), packaged inside a squirrel or a stoat.

But one of their ideas that really inspired me was to sell shares in their company to the people who love drinking their beer, becoming a plc. They raised around £642,000 to build a new eco-brewery but, most excitingly, recruited a couple of thousand dedicated fans to the team. Their shareholders love their brand and, of course, want to see it succeed—so the company plans to encourage them to ask their local pub to stock BrewDog, tell all their friends about the brand and generally send in their ideas for how they can take over the world of beer!

4 Researching and Pitching Your Idea

You might spend years on developing your product, tinkering away in your garden shed perfecting a prototype to show to your first big potential customers. On the other hand, you might well have everything in place to start approaching customers within a few weeks, depending on what kind of product or service you've come up with. No matter what business idea you have, there are a few lessons I've learned from the long and difficult journey of getting SuperJam into the major supermarkets, which will help you through the process of researching and pitching your idea to move to the next stage of getting your product out there.

Getting to Know the Competition

In my mind, you should begin the process of developing your product by trying to understand everything you can about your customers and also everything you can about what the competition is already doing. That way, you can get a picture of what your customer wants from your product that the competition isn't quite delivering on; that will be what you might call your 'unique selling point'.

In reality, the world is full of millions of products so you don't need to worry too much about yours being truly unique. But you will certainly have to offer your customers one simple and compelling reason for buying your brand over the competition.

It is really easy to find out what your competitors are up to: they're shouting about it in their advertising and press coverage! Try the products yourself, read articles about them, visit their stores, talk to their staff and download their company accounts. You should try to understand where each of your competitors sits in the market. Who makes the most money and why? What kind of people buy their products? Try to figure out what they do well and what they don't do so well.

Understanding Your Customers

Understanding your customers isn't always quite as easy. You will need to build an image in your mind of who is likely to buy your product and where the bulk of your sales will come from. It could be housewives or it might be sausage factories, it will depend on your product.

There's a fair chance that the first prototype you make won't hit the nail on the head; show it to people and see what they think you should change. You should do everything you can to perfect your concept before taking it to market. It's a huge amount easier to make changes now compared to when your brand is on the shelves.

Try to spend time with your potential customers, understanding why they buy the brand they do at the moment. Is it because it is good value for money or because it is reliable? You need to talk to them, asking what they think is missing from the brand and what they wished it would do. What would make them use more of it? Maybe they think it should be in the colour blue, that it should come in a bigger container, or that it should be cheaper. All of this information will give you a picture of what your product needs to be.

Getting the Pricing Right

Coming up with a price for your product will be one of the defining decisions that you make and it shouldn't be taken lightly. Once you have launched your brand at a certain price, it is usually very difficult to change it, especially if you are supplying big companies. The only direction the buyers want your price to go is down.

It goes without saying that to get a sense of what you should be charging for your product, you're going to have to be competitive against what other people are charging. But the challenge will be making sure that you can make a decent margin at that price; if not, perhaps you're going to need to rethink some part of your concept, otherwise you could launch at a price that is so low you won't have a business for long.

There are all kinds of approaches that you can take to pricing other than simply charging something similar to what the competition does. You can think about blowing the competition out of the water by giving your product or service away for free; why not try to make money from selling advertising or upgrades to premium versions? Look at the *Metro* newspaper or Google, for example, brands that we come in contact with every day without paying a penny.

If you have a good picture of what you think the customer is going to be willing to pay for your product, you'll be in a good position when it comes to negotiating with manufacturers and figuring out if you stand to make a profit when you find out what it costs to produce.

What you'll be able to charge for your products will have a lot to do with where you plan on selling them. Whatever price you decide to offer your product at will determine what kind of outlets will be interested in stocking your brand and which ones won't. Getting the price right will be critical to the success of your brand.

Finding Outlets for Your Product

In my case the most logical place to start selling SuperJam was supermarkets and up-market independent stores, but you might want to sell direct on your own website, through a catalogue, on home shopping channels or on a market stall. The benefits of selling through a large retailer like Waitrose are that you can reach almost every postcode in the country right away, millions of people walk past your product on the shelves every week (hopefully some of them stop and pick it up!) and the volumes can be astronomical.

Having said that, there is something beautiful about having a direct relationship with your customer, something that can be lost if you sell through someone else's stores. The closer you are to your customers, the more you can understand them and hopefully that can help you to improve what you are offering.

There's a lot to be said for focusing on one market before trying to take over the world, so try to figure out where the easiest place is going to be for you to sell in order to get your product off the ground. I'm a big believer in starting small, maybe even on a market stall or by selling online to start with, to let you test the waters before leaping in.

Researching My Super Idea

Having left school at the age of 16 so that I could cook jam in my parents' tiny kitchen all day every day, I soon found myself cooking up to 1,000 jars of homemade jam every week, selling them at farmers' markets and to small shops all over Scotland.

It soon got to the point where my parents simply couldn't get into the kitchen to cook the dinner any more and I realized that if I wanted to grow my business any further, I would need to come up with a big idea in order to make the leap into factory production.

So I began doing a lot of research, online and by getting market research reports from the library, only to discover that the jam market was in a dismal state.

Sales had been in decline for decades, mostly because jam is usually incredibly unhealthy, sometimes containing 70% or even 80% sugar, but also because it has a very old-fashioned image. Usually when people think of jam, they think of old women and church fêtes.

I decided that I was going to set myself the ambition of changing all of that. It became an obsession and I researched jam in every way I could. I'd read recipe books and experiment in my parent's tiny kitchen for days on end, sometimes staying up all night if I thought I was on to something. If friends went on holiday to an exotic place, I'd ask them to bring home jam for me to try. I wanted to reinvent the world of jam by coming up with a healthier and more modern brand.

I began to focus more and more on the idea of making jam entirely from fruit, without adding any sugar at all. I tried making jam sweetened with honey, but it proved too expensive and I didn't like the consistency. I tried adding fruits that were particularly sweet, experimenting with all kinds of processes and endless different cooking times.

One afternoon, after literally hundreds of batches and dozens of failed concepts, I created a batch of jam entirely from fruit and fruit juice. It tasted beautiful, really fruity and natural, the way jam is supposed to be.

Having come up with the recipe, I was now more excited than ever that I could reinvent the world of jam and reverse the fortunes of the industry.

And that was the birth of SuperJam.

Of course, before I could start banging down the doors of supermarkets or any other kind of retailer, I had to give some thought to how I planned to get the word out about my brand and beat the existing jam brands at their own game.

Getting Your Brand Out There

It's all very well putting something out into the world that is the best thing since sliced bread at a bargain price, but if nobody knows about it, you're going nowhere. So, right from the start, you're going to have to develop a clear plan for promoting your business.

You should really be looking into promotion methods that are very different to what your competitors are already doing. You might even be able to reinvigorate your industry, by attracting people to buy your products who wouldn't normally even consider buying from your competitors.

You're the new guy in town, and you have the innovative new product that is going to take over the market and beat the incumbent players at their game. Stand out from all of them by talking in a different tone in your marketing materials, don't take yourself too seriously and do everything you can to relate to your customers. You know the reasons they have for not buying your kind of product in the past, so talk to them about how you've solved their gripe. 'Don't you just hate how this product only ever comes in blue? Well, so did we, until we set up our own business offering it in every colour of the rainbow.'

There are all kinds of types of promotions that you can consider using to tell people about your brand: advertising, money-off promotions, sampling, PR and events. I'm going to talk in more depth about all of them later in the book but, at this stage, you should have an idea about what you think will work for your brand. You'll need to convince buyers or investors to believe in your idea and if you don't have a good promotional plan, they know that you'll be dead in the water. And the best way to get buyers, investors, banks or anyone else on board is to show them what you plan to do to make your business work.

Writing a Business Plan

Once you've come up with an idea, there's a lot to be said for writing down all of your aspirations and ideas in a plan, backed up by the research that you have done into why anyone will ever buy your product.

You will need to write a convincing business plan if you hope to raise bank funding, grants and, of course, investment from outsiders. Although it might seem tedious, by putting your ideas down on paper, you can clarify them in your own mind as well. If you are totally honest about the shortcomings of each aspect of the idea, you will hopefully be pretty sure of what you need to work on.

I've never written a massive business plan with dozens and dozens of pages. It can be easy to get bogged down planning and researching your idea. There is a risk that if you keep planning, you'll end up never getting the business started. You should bear in mind that the people you're going to be showing your business plan to are likely to be very busy. So it will be in your best interests to keep the document as short and simple as possible.

In your business plan, there are four things that you need to cover, explaining them as clearly and simply as you can:

1. *The benefits of your product over the alternatives.* Why should anyone buy it?
2. *Who is going to buy your product.* Where will it be sold and what kind of person will end up spending their hard-earned money on it?
3. *That the commercial elements stack up.* Is the pricing competitive? Will you and your retailers both make a decent margin?
4. *What you are going to do to get the name out there.* How do you plan on promoting your business and getting those vital first orders?

In my experience, if you can explain those four things clearly and demonstrate truthfully that your product stacks up on all fronts, you will be able to put together a business plan that gives a bank, investor or anyone else faith in your idea.

Once you've finished writing your business plan and you've done everything you can to develop your product ready for the market, it might well be time to pitch your idea. This could be to a retailer or investor, or to whoever else it is that you need to convince to make the whole thing happen. You're really going to have to prepare and know everything you can about the market, your product and how you're going to promote your brand, and do your best to get them excited about the journey ahead of you.

Pitching Your Product

Throughout the development of your business, you will no doubt have to pitch your ideas, your products and yourself to customers, bankers, investors or any number of other people who can hopefully help you take things to the next level. You're going to be invited to share your story with them, telling them about what you've done to get to where you are now, what the plans are for the future and how you want them to help you get there.

Whoever you are pitching to, they will no doubt be extremely busy, especially if you're trying to show your products to the buyer for a large retailer.

The first step, of course, will be to make contact with the buyer, which is sometimes easier said than done. Find out who the buyer is by calling the retailer's head office. Send them some samples of your product and a simple outline of your story, what you're planning to do and how you're going to make your product sell in their stores. Of course, if you have any testimonials or press clippings, send them along too.

Give the buyer a couple of weeks to have a chance to look at what you've sent them and follow up with a phone call; ask if you can come and meet them to tell them more about your product. With any luck, they'll invite you in to pitch for their business.

Now's your big chance, so make sure you do your homework. Don't write a great speech or expect to be presenting to a hundred people; it is most likely going to be you telling your story to one or two buyers, which isn't as scary as you might imagine.

What to Cover in Your Pitch

- ♦ *A brief history of the business.* How you came up with the idea and where you are now.
- ♦ *The features and benefits of your product.* How it compares with the competition.
- ♦ *What you're going to do to promote the brand.* Perhaps you will pay for money-off promotions for their customers or advertising in their magazine.
- ♦ *As much commercial information as you can.* The number of products in the range, the price they should roughly retail for and what margins the retailer can expect.

Whoever you are pitching to will no doubt have plenty of questions about how you plan on promoting the brand, what you're doing to generate publicity around the launch and so on. Hopefully, if you do a good job of telling them everything they need to know, they'll be willing to give it a shot. This could be on a trial basis in a few stores, or they might just take on one of your products and see how it performs.

Pitching to Waitrose

In the newspaper one day, I read that the much-loved British supermarket chain 'The Food Stores of the John Lewis Partnership', Waitrose, was to open its first two stores in Scotland.

They would be in Edinburgh, my home town, and the company was encouraging local food producers to come along to an event; a 'Meet The Buyer Day', to pitch their ideas to the supermarket's most senior buyers.

I figured that this would be my big break and I wanted to do everything I could to impress Waitrose. I saw it as the perfect outlet for my product, since its ethos was supporting small suppliers.

The type of people who shop at Waitrose generally have a little extra money to spend on premium food products. I figured that they were probably likely to be interested in SuperJam, because it was an upmarket brand of 100% fruit jams.

I was pretty nervous about pitching my ideas to Waitrose, as I felt like I had entered 'The X-Factor of Supplying Groceries to Supermarkets'. I felt like one of those amateur singers who stands in a line with hundreds of others waiting to give the five-minute performance that might just change their life.

The only difference was that the people in this queue were holding boxes of homemade cakes and chutneys, and some had brought vegetables from their small farms or beer from their microbrewery.

After what felt like a decade, my time came and I walked into a small room where sat the senior jam buyer, a friendly guy by the name of Michael Simpson-Jones.

He waited patiently as I told him how I had learned to make jam with my gran, my early successes of selling my home-made produce at farmers markets and to local shops, and about all of the research I had done. I listed all of the statistics I had read about the decline in jam sales, presented SuperJam as the solution to jam's unpopularity and offered him the chance to try my homemade jams.

I explained that SuperJam was better than what was already on the shelves of his stores because it was made entirely from fruit and was all natural. I told him that I thought the brand would appeal to exactly the type of people who shop in Waitrose, people who earn good money and enjoy eating well. I also gave him an idea of what I thought SuperJam should retail for and what Waitrose might expect to make from it. It also seemed like a good idea to tell him all about my ideas for how we could promote the brand: that I would be happy to stand in some of the stores, handing out samples and telling people all about the products myself.

After listening to my pitch and trying everything I had brought along, Mike explained that, although it was very refreshing for him to see a teenager coming along with a dream to reinvent the world of jam, there was a long way to go until I would have a product that could sit on the shelves of a leading supermarket like Waitrose. I'd have to set up production in a factory and be able to produce SuperJam at a competitive price. I would have to create a brand that people loved and do a lot more work on my recipes before he would be happy.

Although there was a long way to go, Mike promised that if I could do a good job of those three things, I'd be welcome to go back, in say a year, and he'd consider launching the products in Waitrose stores.

I reflected on everything that he had suggested to me. The challenge of getting SuperJam into Waitrose stores was going to be much bigger than I had imagined. I had no idea how I was going to convince a factory to work with me or how I would go about creating a brand that people would love. But with such great feedback about the overall concept from the buyer, I figured that these were challenges I could overcome, and I committed to giving it a shot. So on the back of that meeting, I decided to put everything I had into trying to create a product that Waitrose would be happy with.

Creating the Brand

By that time I was a student at the University of Strathclyde, studying Accountancy and Marketing. Obviously, as a student and a teenager, I didn't have access to a huge amount of money to fund the creation of the SuperJam brand.

I contacted a number of design agencies around Scotland and some in London, telling them all about my idea to reinvent the world of jam. I asked for a quote to create the SuperJam branding: the logo, the packaging, the website and some promotional materials such as leaflets and posters.

Soon the quotes started to trickle back. Some were £10,000, others £20,000 and some were even as much as £40,000! Needless to say, the quotes were all a lot more than I could afford.

Eventually, I came across a local advertising agency called IASmarts, who mostly worked on advertising for huge companies and the government and won a lot of awards for what it produced. The director of the company said that it was a really fun idea and a project that he figured his designers would enjoy working on.

He also really believed in the SuperJam idea, so he agreed to work on my branding for free, as long as I gave the agency some repeat business if everything became the huge success that we all hoped it would be.

Super Heroes

All fired up about the prospect of working together to create the next big thing in the world of jam, the designers and I sat down and had a think about what the packaging should look like.

The head designer, a mega talented and witty guy called Simon Shaw, came up with the thought that there was a link between 'SuperJam' and 'SuperMan', so we began to develop the concept of creating a super hero-style brand. It was an idea that I loved.

We had a huge amount of fun writing jokes on the labels and we excitedly spoke of creating a superheroesque costume for me, the 'Jam Boy', to wear at the launch of the whole thing.

The leaflets were designed to look like a comic book, with the 'Jam Boy' character coming to the rescue in Jam Land. The website was to be equally wacky.

Having come up with a brand that I thought was super funny and really cool, I began work on solving the small problem of how I was going to produce hundreds of thousands of jars of SuperJam to sell to the big supermarkets.

Finding a Factory

Of course, as a teenager I didn't have enough money lying around to build my own jam factory. I also wasn't realistically in a position to ask a bank to lend me that kind of money either.

So I was going to have to convince an existing jam factory to work with me to produce SuperJam on a big scale. This was a search that would prove to be a lot more challenging than I immediately thought. Not only was I going to have to convince a factory to work with me, I was going to have to give its owners good reason to risk their resources backing my idea.

Since I had so little finance behind me, I was going to have to find a factory willing to put up the working capital to buy fruit, jars and labels to make the first batch of tens of thousands of jars. I would then agree with the factory that they would be paid back for all of that initial outlay, plus their margin, as soon as we had sold the finished product to the supermarkets. The factory would also have to wait to be paid until the supermarket had paid me; typically a month or two after we delivered the jam to them.

All in all, I was asking them to risk £50,000 or maybe even £100,000 on my idea, with no guarantee that they would ever see a penny of it again.

So I travelled around the country, from the tiny islands off the north coast of Scotland to the big cities of England, trying to find someone to work with me to produce this SuperJam.

As you can probably imagine, most of these huge food companies, some of them publicly listed on the stock market, were somewhat sceptical of a teenager showing up with no money, no experience and in fact nothing more than just some recipes and a vague ambition to transform the world of jam.

Although most of the jam factories were not willing to give my ideas a shot, I came across one that had suffered from the decline in jam sales, had a lot of spare capacity and figured that, just maybe, SuperJam would be the answer to their problems. Its owners were excited about my idea because I had told them about how much Waitrose liked the concept and my story.

A few months later and after some successful and not-so-successful factory trials, they had figured out how to make SuperJam on the large scale I needed in order to supply Waitrose.

I decided I was ready to go back to Mike and pitch the final concepts to him.

Pitching Again

I showed the new labels to Mike and told him about the factory I had found to produce the range. I gave him an indication of the price at which we would be able to sell the products to him, and the price at which we would end up retailing on the shelf.

Although Mike still liked the idea of making jam entirely from fruit, he explained to me that the fact that SuperJam was so healthy had been completely lost in the humour of the comic book labels.

He explained that the factory I had chosen to work with would end up being far too expensive and he didn't really like the flavours we had come up with either. Basically, everything I had spent a year working on would have to be thrown in the bin!

When Waitrose also turned down the labels that we had created, I learned how crucial the design of products is to their success. People don't really buy products because they look cool or funny, they buy them because the packaging communicates really clearly why they should. The labels we had created didn't do a very good job of telling people that SuperJam was all fruit and all natural; it was probably so colourful that it didn't look very natural at all.

It was very clear how important it was going to be to look after the costs of making the product, otherwise we could end up sitting on the shelf with a price ticket much higher than people would be willing to pay. I wanted SuperJam to be a brand that people could buy every week and feel it was good value for money.

The response from Waitrose was terrible news. Not only was I disappointed by it, but the factory and designers were devastated that all of the hard work they had put in was going to be thrown away. The designers were really proud of the comic book labels and were sad to see them go. When it became clear that it wasn't going to be possible for me to continue working with the factory, because they worked out to be too expensive, they were upset no longer to be a part of the SuperJam adventure.

That was probably the lowest point of the whole adventure, the moment when I wasn't sure if it would ever work, when I asked myself if I had been wasting my time all along.

Family and friends admitted that this is where they probably would have given up. 'You've put six months into this and it hasn't worked out, so why not cut your losses and try something new?'. Everyone who was supporting me was wondering whether this was the end of the SuperJam dream.

Picking Myself Up to Try Again

You've probably already guessed what happened next.

Although things hadn't really worked out, I still completely believed in the idea of reinventing the world of jam. I took Waitrose's comments on board as advice for how I could make SuperJam even better. All I had to do was create a brand that was a lot simpler and would get the message across more clearly. I also needed to set up production in a factory that could meet Waitrose's quality but also come in at a competitive price and really perfect the recipes.

I took a deep breath and decided that I would be short changing myself if I didn't do what I believed in and give the idea another shot.

In getting your business off the ground, you can be sure that there will be moments when things don't work, when people let you down or you face rejection. Starting a business isn't easy and it is moments like these that show you what makes it so hard. There will be moments when you consider giving up, when you want to walk away from your idea because you can't quite see how to overcome the challenge you face. But I can assure you that when you try again, find a way forward and make everything work out, the feeling at the end will be all the more satisfying.

Solving the Branding Problem

I met again with the designer, Simon, who had created the super hero branding. He was pretty devastated by the news that the comic book idea, his 'baby', hadn't captured the minds of the supermarket buyers in the same way as it had ours.

We spent some time trying to figure out what had gone wrong and realized that we had never really asked ourselves what our target market would want and expect SuperJam to look like.

'Who is going to buy SuperJam?' was the question that we should have been asking ourselves all along. We clarified to ourselves that it wasn't kids and teenagers, my friends, who may well have found the comic book idea funny: it was adults.

We'd have a matter of seconds to communicate to the supermarket shopper why they should buy SuperJam. We needed to decide in our own minds exactly why they should and how we could tell them.

Around this time, I visited the headquarters of Innocent, 'Fruit Towers' as it is called, one of my all-time favourite companies. They were in the relatively early days of taking over the world of fruit smoothies, and their packaging, ethics and the way they were so open with the consumer massively inspired me.

I was lucky enough to meet with a guy called Dan Germain, who was responsible for creating the Innocent brand. His view was that packaging should talk to consumers in the same way as friends talk to one another down the pub.

He hated the way that big food companies spoke about how 'your statutory rights are not affected' on their packaging and talked to consumers without having any personality and without being straight-forward.

He also spoke about the fact that the most enduring grocery brands, like Marmite, Heinz ketchup, Campbell's soup and Coca-Cola, don't change the look and feel of their brand with fashion, they stay consistent. By being so consistent, they remain brands we love, brands we remember from childhood and brands we trust.

I think probably one of the best pieces of advice anyone has given me was from Dan. He said that a brand should only have one thing it wants to say. It should say it in a really simple way and keep saying it over and over again.

Armed with this advice, I realized that, like Innocent, our message should be '100% fruit' and that we should aim to create a brand and packaging that got that message across really simply.

Having taking this new approach, Simon came up with a number of different ideas for the packaging and ultimately we settled on the branding that you see on the products today. The labels are very simple and mostly white, with a clear description of the product inside and some nice colourful patterns to bring them to life. No pictures of farms or of the fruits themselves, which is so common in jam brands. And no superheroes!

Finding a New Factory

Now that we had packaging that everyone was happy with, I set out to find a new factory. This time, I would need to find a factory that could make the products to Waitrose's high standards and be able to cut some costs from the process so that we could offer the buyer a price that would work.

I travelled around the country a bit more, knocking on the doors of 150-year-old family businesses who had been making jam for generations. 'How could this kid from Scotland have possibly come up with an idea we haven't?' was no doubt how they felt.

When I was beginning to doubt whether anyone would ever work with me, I came across a factory that specialized in making high-quality own-brand jams for the likes of Waitrose and Marks & Spencer. I met with a guy called David Smith, who knew just about everything there was to know about the jam industry and he got really excited about my idea.

He invited me for a tour of their factory. It was very Willy Wonka and, for me, an amazing sight. When I visited, in the height of summer, they were making hundreds of thousands of jars of mincemeat: the whole place smelled like Christmas!

It was much bigger and more efficient than the previous factory and had machines for putting labels onto jars and jars into cases. At the previous place, jobs like that were done by hand. Seeing the labelling equipment was almost heart-breaking: watching a machine do in seconds what used to take me an afternoon in my parents' kitchen.

Des and his team set to work right away on figuring out how his factory could work with me to make SuperJam on a big scale and at a price that would work for the supermarkets. They had never made a product as complex as SuperJam. Not adding any sugar makes it a lot trickier to get the jam to set, especially when you're making thousands of jars at a time.

Eventually, we had figured out how to produce SuperJam at a price that we could offer Waitrose, leaving enough margin to cover promotional costs, distribution and hopefully profit for the factory and for me.

The Final Pitch

We presented the new packaging designs and our prices to the Waitrose buyer, who absolutely loved the clean, modern and simple design of the packaging and said that we were 'almost there' on the pricing.

The buyer explained that, at the cost we had suggested to him, the retail price of a jar of SuperJam would end up at almost £2.50, when realistically it should be £1.50 if we wanted to be competitive with other brands of jam in the category.

I wasn't willing to compromise on the quality of SuperJam, so we had to figure out how to get about 50p of cost out of each jar, while maintaining the best-tasting and healthiest jam possible.

The factory suggested that if I was able to commit to producing really large batches of jam at a time, something like 50,000 jars, there would be some considerable cost savings. This was mostly because if the factory can make one big batch of jam a day instead of lots of smaller ones, there is less time wasted between batches on cleaning equipment.

It was a huge gamble to consider, because I would be liable for stumping up the cash for the cost of producing 50,000 jars if they didn't sell. However, it also meant that I'd be able to go back to Waitrose with a price it would be happy with. We would be competitive with other brands in the market, the supermarket would make a decent margin and so would the factory. With all this in mind, I took this as my last shot, and agreed with the factory to push the 'Go' button.

5 Launch!

Now you're on the home straight. You have everything in place to launch your new product or service. You just need the next few steps to go smoothly and you'll have made it to your goal of getting your idea to market.

The products are fully developed, the finishing touches to the branding have been added and you have that first big order. You can almost taste the excitement in the air. Everyone around you is delighted that you've almost made it.

The challenge you have now is to let everyone know that you're open for business, that you're up and running and that they're welcome to come and say hello. If you've opened a physical shop, you'll have to tell everyone in the area; that might mean handing out flyers, advertising in the local paper and offering a special promotion to get people to come in and try you out.

If you're launching online, this is your chance to get bloggers to write about you and link to your site; send samples or offer them the chance to try out your service. You're also going to need to consider the best Google Adwords to buy and other ways of promoting your business both online and off.

If you're bringing a physical product into the world, you will have to seize the moment to get as many people caught up in the launch buzz as possible. You're only going to be the new kid in town for a few weeks, until something else comes along that everyone wants to read about. Don't delay in sending out samples of your products to influential people, handing out freebies at all the right events and making sure that everyone who has registered an interest in your product gets all the information they need for them to want to buy one.

It is important to keep your eye on the ball for the next few months. If something goes wrong with the first production run, for example, the whole thing might fall through. How you decide to go about launching your product is critical because it will be your first impression on the public, the media and your customers; you want it to be as positive as possible.

Start Small

The year or so after the launch of SuperJam was the most exciting period of my life up to that point. What made it so exciting was partly the fact that things were going well, that everything I had worked towards for years was beginning to happen. As well as this, what made it exciting was that it was very risky. If things hadn't gone so well, I could have gone bankrupt.

A lot depends on the business you're looking to start, the economies of scale involved and the type of customers you're trying to attract. In a lot of cases, the best way to get things off the ground is to start on a small scale. Often, people don't get past the starting point because they're aiming too high.

There's no need to try to take over the world from day one. A lot of the time, the best thing to do is to make a small batch of your product or offer your service to a small group of potential customers. Once that is a success, you can cast your net a bit wider and continue to grow in manageable chunks.

Launching on a small scale limits risks because it takes less investment than trying to launch on a huge scale. It gives you a chance to try out your idea before investing a lot of money in producing a huge amount of your product, or taking on employees to deliver your services. At this stage, the more you can do yourself the better, until you are totally sure that your product is solid and the business has the potential to make money.

If you are starting your business at the weekends and in the evenings after work, then launching on a small scale will probably make a lot of sense. This could mean only offering your product in a local area to start with, or to a select group of people who you think will love the idea. There's nothing worse than people launching a product and then not being able to keep up with demand.

You can see if the idea works and then scale up gradually, hopefully one day taking the leap and devoting more of your time to it, perhaps leaving your job to focus on your business full time, or raising the funds needed to turn your fledgling enterprise into a fully formed business, employing people and manufacturing products at scale.

Even though you might well start out on a small scale, you should always maintain a picture of where you ultimately want to take the business. No doubt you will want it to grow and move into bigger premises, employ people and launch a wider range of products. By keeping that in mind and always being focused on what is important to you, you'll be able to make the right decisions to help you get there.

In my case, starting on a small scale by producing jam at home and selling it at farmers' markets and to small shops gave me a very valuable opportunity to learn all about the market. I understood what people wanted from jam, what frustrated them about it; mostly that it contained heaps of unhealthy sugar. They made comments about every aspect of what I was doing, giving feedback on my labels, pricing and recipes. I took on board what they said about my original products and packaging and was ultimately able to develop a mainstream brand and set up production on a larger scale in a factory, as you have seen.

Building a Website

There is no doubt that you should have a website for your business, no matter what you're selling. It might be a few simple pages telling people about your product or it might be a full ecommerce site that allows people to order online. Whatever you need from your site, you should definitely have it up and running and looking great in time for the launch of your product. As soon as people hear about your new product, it'll be the first place they head to for more information, so make sure it's ready for them!

Your website should be as simple and easy to use as possible and really explain your product to people in a matter of seconds. In the same way as designing good packaging, you really have to grab their interest. I personally think that using videos and lots of pictures, rather than pages and pages of words, is the best way to get your message across.

When you're building your website, you should take every opportunity to try to open up a conversation with the people who are interested in your brand. That means having a blog that you update as regularly as possible, links to your Twitter and Facebook pages and videos from you, the founder. All of this helps to capture some of your passion for the topic.

I also think that you should allow people either to pre-order your product or at least to register their interest on the website, even if they are going to have to wait for a few weeks or months. There will always be people who love your idea so much that they want to get their hands on it before anyone else. If you can't take pre-orders for your product, you should definitely collect people's emails with a 'register your interest here' page. That way, you can get back in touch with them once you're up and running; hopefully these people who have expressed an interest in your concept will become some of your first few customers.

It is critical to the success of your brand that you take every opportunity to connect with your customers. I'm going to talk about how SuperJam has been able to do that later on in the book, particularly how we've used our website to engage with the people buying our products, but first let's look at the website itself.

The SuperJam Website

We set up a new website designed in the same style as the SuperJam labels. The site also included a blog, which I have since updated every few days with news, stories and ideas. This has proven to be a very powerful way of engaging with SuperJam customers, gaining thousands of regular readers and hundreds of thousands of visitors. We receive a lot of orders on the website, even though it isn't a massive part of the overall business. I think that this success is down to the website being very simple, clean and focusing only on the information that is important: the product range we have, where you can get it from, how much it is, and how to get in touch. You won't find pages and pages of text on there.

On my blog, I write about my ideas, thoughts and generally what I have recently been doing to develop the business. Visitors to the site can follow the story as it develops and also post comments, sharing their own views on my ideas and the products.

Of course, the importance of your website on launch day will depend a lot on the type of business you're starting. If your company is only selling online, it is obviously going to be crucial that the website is up and running in time for your launch.

Beta Launch

In software companies, a usual part of the product launch is to have a 'beta launch' before making the website or application available to the general public. The company will allow a select group of consumers or businesses that they trust to use the software. The customers might get to use the product for free or at a heavily reduced price, so that the company can see how well the system works and hopefully gets valuable feedback from this small group of users.

By launching the product with an enthusiastic group of initial customers who are excited to have 'exclusive' access, you can create a lot of buzz around the launch. A writer called Kevin Kelly wrote about an idea he had that, rather than trying to 'make it big', artistes could focus their energies on nurturing a fan base of their 1,000 truest fans, the people who love their music and are willing to drive across the country to hear them play. By creating music for that group of people, engaging with them and listening to what they say, the artiste can create a very loyal following who are willing to pay good money for what they produce. He suggested that an artiste who has 1,000 true fans could well make a better living than one who is trying to appeal to millions.

I love the idea of finding the 1,000 or so people who are most excited about your idea and letting them be the people who get to try it out first. If they really love the concept, they will be more than happy to give you bucketloads of feedback and ideas. And what is more, when you finally release the product to the public, you'll have used their feedback to make sure that it is spot on. There will be so much mystery and buzz around your product because of the exclusivity you have created that people will hopefully be desperate to get their hands on it. You can maybe even let the 'beta testers' choose the next set of people to try it out, by inviting their friends. At the very least, you can use them to promote the launch to their friends and connections, online and offline.

Whether your business is based online or off, it's going to be important that you get out there in the real world and meet potential customers. You need to promote what you're doing to all the right people, to give your business the best possible chance to get off the ground.

Trade Fairs

Whatever industry you're in, there is probably at least one related trade show for it. So you might want to consider using this as an opportunity to launch your product. You can find out about suitable trade fairs by asking people in your industry which ones they go to, or by searching the web; they tend to be promoted quite widely.

All of the relevant people for your particular industry, whether it's cushions or software or potatoes, are likely to be at the trade show, so if you make enough buzz around your launch by getting the event organizers to promote it in the show brochures and on their website, you could potentially get a huge amount of business from it. Stands at trade fairs and other big events can be very expensive, hundreds or maybe even thousands of pounds, but don't be afraid to negotiate with the event organizers. You can sometimes score yourself a bargain, especially at the last minute.

Even if you don't use a trade show as a platform to launch your product, they can be a great place to promote your brand to the right kind of people. Whether you buy a stand or not, you can mingle with the other exhibitors and find out their thoughts on the market. You might find that it is a good place to search for advice, connections and maybe even a mentor. Don't be frightened of going up to exhibitors and asking them all about their product and story. Who did they speak to at Tesco? What are the challenges in their business? Who is their biggest customer? The information they give you could well be like gold dust.

Launch Party!

I think having a launch party for your new business is a great idea. It's an opportunity to mark the start of your business, the point where it all becomes real. It's a chance to thank some of the people who made it possible and, of course, to tell the press all about your story. You can also invite along some of your first customers and suppliers, potential customers and maybe even some celebrities.

What is appropriate for your launch party is entirely down to what your product is. But no matter what you're launching, the event should almost certainly be free to attend for the people you invite, especially the press. You should also bear in mind that the press and celebrities you might hope to attract to your launch are invited to dozens of similar events every week. You are going to need a novel idea for your event, to make it exciting enough for the right kind of people to want to come along.

That hook might be the venue or it could be an interesting speaker you have invited along. Maybe you'll have a live band or some delicious food and drink. Make sure that your event is suitable for the message you are trying to get across. You might want to try to limit the amount you spend on it by getting a sponsor on board or partnering with another brand.

When SuperJam launched, we had an event in my local Waitrose store in Edinburgh. The store manager was very proud that they were able to promote a local business and they made a massive display of jars of SuperJam. The press came along and people drove from 60 miles away to come and see the launch of the brand. It was a massive success and I think we sold something like 1,500 jars of SuperJam on that first day, which was more jam than that store usually sold in a month. In fact, I think it got to the point where if anyone tried to go through the checkout and hadn't bought a jar of SuperJam, the person sat at the checkout would ask why not! It was a fantastic moment to realize that SuperJam had finally arrived.

Announcing the Launch

There is a whole range of things that you can do to announce the launch of your brand and probably at the top of the list is writing a press release. It is one way of telling journalists about your story and, if you do it well, could get you some serious coverage.

Journalists receive literally hundreds of press releases every day, for all kinds of different stories. The trick is to figure out how to get them excited about your story in the first few sentences. Giving them the essence of what the story is should help to grab their attention. For example, 'Eleanor Brown, a Portsmouth grandmother, will bake the world's biggest brownie this Saturday, to launch her new bakery Ellie's Cakes', will make them want to read on.

Overall, you want your press release to be fairly short. Nobody wants to read pages and pages about your product launch, especially not journalists. Tell them a bit about your background, how you came up with the idea and what successes you have had to date. Make the release more human by including a few quotes: from yourself, your first few customers and anyone else you think might add colour to the story. You only really need to write enough to give the journalist a good overview of your story and make them curious to read more and, hopefully, to want to interview you.

It is crucial that your press release doesn't simply read like an advert; who would want to read that? It has to be newsworthy, accurate and mustn't exaggerate.

You're going to have to get your press release out as far and wide as possible, and ideally at the same time. You also want the story to go to print at the same time in every newspaper and magazine that chooses to write about it. This might mean telling magazines about it a month before you tell newspapers, due to their differing copy deadlines. You can find out this kind of information by getting in touch with the publications and asking them about the timescales they work towards. As soon as your story is printed it becomes old news, so if you aren't careful with the timings, you will end up being written about in only one or two places, which is likely to make little impact.

You can send your release directly to journalists and newspapers by locating their email addresses from their websites. I'd also recommend checking out press release distribution websites, some of which are focused on news specific to a local area, to help get the release in front of the right people.

If you have the budget to, you might also want to consider taking on a PR agency to help you promote the story. You can expect to spend £1,000–2,000 a month for one, or more if you want them to do a lot of work. Perhaps you could employ their services only for the first couple of months of your business, to help with the launch.

You want to pick the agency that 'gets' your story and is most excited about working with you. They are going to be calling up journalists on your behalf, telling them your story. There would be nothing worse than an unenthusiastic agent calling up the journalists to tell them about it when they don't really believe in the idea themselves. The journalists would smell the insincerity a mile off and, chances are, you wouldn't get a lot of press. But if you can find a PR agency that really loves your brand, they'll sound truly authentic when they speak to the press about you and will probably even go the extra mile to help get publicity. It can work really well if you find an agency filled with people who you really like and who really like you.

Since I didn't have much budget to pay for advertising, a PR agency or anything like that, media coverage of my story was going to be a very powerful way of raising the profile of SuperJam.

I had no idea how to get my story out to journalists and so Waitrose suggested that, in exchange for six months' exclusivity of SuperJam, it would help to promote the story. This sounded like a very fair deal to me, so we granted exclusivity to Waitrose for the first six months. The first production run went smoothly and the first order of 12,000 jars was delivered safely to the Waitrose warehouse, ready for the launch. A few weeks later the products went onto the shelves and I was able to act out my dream of buying the first jar myself. I went along to my local Waitrose first thing in the morning and felt very proud seeing all of the jars of SuperJam lined up on the shelves. As part of the exclusive deal, Waitrose was to promote the brand heavily to its shoppers in the in-store magazine, on the shelves and also, most importantly, by sending out a press release to the national press.

Little did I know at this point quite how my story would capture the imagination of the international media.

6 Telling a Story

On the first day that SuperJam launched on the shelves, the first few articles about SuperJam appeared in the Scottish papers. By the afternoon, I was inundated with phone calls from newspapers, radio stations and television producers all wanting to interview me.

Waitrose helped to fuel this media attention by sending out a press release and, over the coming three days, about 30 newspapers and magazines, 16 radio stations and 7 television programmes interviewed me.

This was a completely surreal experience and I couldn't believe how interested people were in the story. Apparently, I was the first teenager ever to supply one of the big supermarkets. This felt like a great achievement. The highlight of all of the media coverage was going on BBC *Breakfast News*. I sat on the couch with the two presenters and chatted about SuperJam, in front of millions of viewers, eating jam on toast for breakfast with them. Amazingly, I didn't feel nervous about all of this; it simply didn't feel real.

The number of newspapers and radio stations abroad that had heard about the story also amazed me. CBC Radio, the biggest radio station in Canada, called up and interviewed me. I also had to do my best at giving an interview to a newspaper in South Korea—who would have thought that people in South Korea would be reading about the wee guy from Edinburgh who turned his gran's jam recipe into a business?

As you can no doubt imagine, all of the media coverage made the launch a major success. Within the first eight months, we had sold more than 150,000 jars—a lot more than I ever imagined!

As a result of the huge success of the products, Tesco, one of the biggest retailers in the world, asked if it too could stock the range. Three phone calls later and without me even needing to meet with the buyer, Tesco agreed to launch SuperJam in more than 300 of its stores across the UK. SuperJam went on sale in Tesco eight months after the launch in Waitrose, and this was again covered extensively in the media. I found myself being interviewed by GMTV, the *Financial Times* and loads of radio stations all around the world. The biggest news show in China even covered the story.

I'm often asked how much I think the success of SuperJam has been down to my story—the story of the kid from Scotland who was taught to make jam by his gran and made a business out of it.

I always say that the success of SuperJam is almost entirely down to that story; all I own is a brand and a brand is just a story. I don't own a factory or a patent or anything else, merely a great story that fascinates people.

But the truth is that my story would have been just as compelling had I been a middle-aged man and left a job to start selling jam. It would have been just as compelling if I had been my gran and had started selling jam; in fact, it would have been an even better story!

There is always a story to tell. Whatever age you are, whatever your business is and however you came up with your idea, there is something exciting about it, something that people want to read about. It is a story that people will connect with, a story that will help them to relate to and trust your brand. It helps them to understand where you've come from and where you're trying to go. When people understand the story behind a brand and know about the people who created it, it has so much more meaning for them and becomes a lot more authentic.

You just have to figure out how to tell it.

Knowing What Your Message Is

I suppose the hard thing is knowing what you're trying to say, what your story is. Like all things, the best stories are usually very simple. Of course, it has to be the truth about how you came up with your idea or what motivated you to change the status quo. There is always a 'hook' for journalists to hang an article onto, a reason why your business is interesting enough to write about.

In my case, I have never been very scientific about any of this stuff; I just learned pretty early on that I had a story to tell. Teachers at school would push me up in front of the class and say: 'Fraser, tell everyone about your jam idea.'

I was never afraid of telling people my story; for me it was something that I loved and I wanted people to hear about it. I was having so much fun setting up my company that I wanted all my friends to understand it.

I've never been a particularly confident person, the kind of guy who can walk into a room full of strangers and go around introducing myself. I was never embarrassed about making jam, though, and never scared of telling people about it.

Talking to the Press

There are all sorts of ways in which you can get the press interested in your story. Journalists are always on the look-out for new things to write about and, if you give them a good enough story, you could well become their next article. A great hook for an article could be that you have won an award, like 'the best-tasting chilli sauce in England', or maybe you've won an award for being so innovative. There are hundreds of different competitions for every kind of business, so search them out online and enter as many as you can.

Of course, your product could well be a hook in its own right and the story of how you came to develop the idea might well be fascinating to the press. Although you don't need to tell them all about your personal life, your age or your background could be a hook.

Another great hook for a story could be that you have won a big contract with a retailer or someone else. Often, you can get the retailer's PR department to help you out getting coverage of the story since it will benefit them too, by showing that they are taking on innovative new products and supporting small suppliers.

The key for you is to decide which magazines, newspapers, television shows or blogs would be best for your story and getting in touch to ask for the name of the right journalist to tell your story to. Don't be afraid of picking up the phone to the press; they're always looking for new stories to tell. Send them some samples of your product and let them see for themselves how wonderful it is.

Writing Articles

The media are always looking for entrepreneurs to comment on what's going on in their community, the economy and their industry. I think that so long as you have something worthwhile to add to the topic and are always positive in what you say, this type of media coverage can only be a good thing.

A fantastic idea is to react to news in the media; if there's a big story about a topic related to what you're doing, then write to the local paper with your opinion. Get your name out there and become a spokesperson for your industry. Whenever I am asked to comment on, say, entrepreneurship in Scotland or the future of the jam industry, I only ever speak about my personal experience and don't offer opinions, especially not ones that are critical and could be taken out of context.

I'm quite often asked to write articles about trends or things that are going on in the world of food. For example, in the past couple of years jam has seen something of a renaissance (hurrah!) and I've written a few articles about why I think that might be. I guess the reason is that people are 'going back to basics', taking up homely hobbies like knitting and baking, and making jam somehow fits into that trend.

You could also conduct surveys about issues that are in some way related to your product and send the results to the press. If it makes for an interesting story, they will credit you in the article, and of course the findings of your research will be beneficial to your business.

For example, if you own a fish and chip shop by the seaside, your survey might discover that '80% of people like taking day trips to the seaside'. In the same kind of way, you can write articles and comment on trends. Maybe there's been a rise in people going to the seaside for weekends and you're the very person to explain why.

A classic way to get publicity for your business is to try to set a world record or by doing some kind of publicity stunt. It can be a bit of a cliché, but that's only because papers write stories like that all the time; and with good reason, it makes for interesting reading. You might hold an event around your stunt and invite lots of press and celebrities along. If it's wacky and an amazing enough feat, you could well find yourself on television or being sent all around the world on YouTube.

Giving Good Interviews

When you're being interviewed, especially if it's on television or radio, you really are going to have to know your stuff.

Be well prepared for whatever question the journalists might ask you and be able to explain your story, your idea and how people can find out about your business in a matter of a few sentences. Radio is very fast paced and television even more so; you'll probably have only a minute or two to share your story with the world. Speak clearly and don't try to say too much.

You should avoid coming across as merely an advert for your product or service, otherwise the station will never invite you back. Be as polite as you can and respect the fact that you are a guest on someone else's show.

Having said that, the whole point of doing an interview is that you want to tell people your story, with the hope that they will check out your website or come to your shop or buy your product. The key to getting people to want to buy your product is to describe it to them in a way that connects with their emotions. You want them to imagine themselves using it.

Think of some of the most recent things you have bought for yourself. Did you spend hours looking at all of the different options available, making the best and most rational decision possible? Of course you didn't. Almost every decision we make to buy something is an emotional one; we buy things in an impulsive moment when we think 'I've got to have that!'

So, whenever you're telling people about your product, don't list all of its features and benefits. Nobody cares. Talk about how it fits into their lives, how much fun it'll give them, how much easier their housework will be with it, or whatever. You want to 'lifestyle' the story as you tell it, embellishing it with descriptions and images of what the product is like to use.

Global Student Entrepreneur of the Year

Because of the runaway success of SuperJam and since supplying supermarkets was something that no teenager had ever done before, I was given a few prestigious awards. The one that I am most proud of is Global Student Entrepreneur of the Year.

I had been chosen to represent Britain at the Global Student Entrepreneur Awards, along with 23 other finalists. They had chosen these successful student entrepreneurs from 750 entrants from all around the world.

This was the first time I had met so many other young people with successful businesses and a real passion for starting companies. I was completely blown away by the companies that some of the other students had set up. For example, one guy called Erik from Sweden ran a software company and sold his applications to companies such as McDonald's. Another guy called Brendan ran a company called Ten Minute Media, and made websites for people like Mick Jagger from the Rolling Stones. Another was running the seventh fastest-growing company in Canada! These were all students and we were all about the same age.

The judges asked us each to give a 20-minute presentation about our companies, sharing stories about what we had learned from our experiences and what we wanted to achieve in the future. They asked us questions about our ethics, who had helped us to get started and how we came up with our ideas in the first place.

Given that my company was probably the least high-tech out of all of the contestants, I wasn't very confident that I would be chosen as the winner. However, the judges said that they loved the story of my business and felt that I had the potential to go very far in the future. I was obviously delighted to win and to be named the Global Student Entrepreneur of the Year. Aside from the actual prize, a massive bonus of the event was meeting other young entrepreneurs from around the world, some of whom have since become very good friends of mine.

Speaking at Events

Meeting other entrepreneurs at events like the Global Student Entrepreneur Awards has been one of the big highlights of the journey for me. Speaking at events and sharing the story of your business is a wonderful way of getting your name out there. You are able to have a meaningful dialogue with people who are interested in what you have to say and tell them all about the adventure you're on and where you're trying to go.

Of course, a lot will depend on the kind of business you are starting, but there are bound to be industry conferences you can speak at and colleges and universities are always looking for local businesspeople to share their experiences with students.

I'm invited to speak at universities, conferences, graduation ceremonies and entrepreneur events all over the world. God knows how everyone hears about my story in the first place, but I have been lucky enough to have shared it with audiences in beautiful places like Puerto Rico in the Caribbean, Beijing in China and prestigious universities such as Columbia in New York.

I love the thought that when I go and speak in some tiny little village school in Scotland in the middle of nowhere, there are kids there who have never even been to a city. They haven't seen anybody set up a business and probably have quite narrow aspirations for what they want to do in life. When I share my story with them, I often see a little spark going off in their heads and they think: 'Hey, if he can do that, then so could I!'. I get emails all the time from young people who have seem me speak or read about my story and they have started selling cakes or some other thing. That feels pretty amazing.

People often ask if I was picked on at school for being different. Thankfully, nobody ever did laugh at me. I guess I wouldn't have cared if they had, but probably it was because of how comfortable I was about myself that nobody thought to pick on me for it.

In fact, other kids at school were fascinated by my tiny business. A lot of them had never seen anyone set up a company, so they had all kinds of questions and thought the whole thing was fun; some of them have even gone on to set up their own companies since.

I can definitely recommend speaking at events as a way of meeting people who can help grow your business and of practising speaking in front of groups of people, a skill that can be really valuable in life.

Telling my story is something that I love and you will no doubt find some really fun ways to tell yours. Whatever way you get your name out there, all of this publicity will really help when you try to get into more stores or find more customers for your product. If people have heard you speak at an event or read about you in the paper, they're much more likely to buy your product. Having a good story to tell is what will help you sell your brand to a wider and bigger audience.

7 Sell, Sell, Sell

In a relatively short space of time, SuperJam has gone from being stocked in just over 100 Waitrose stores on the day of launch, to being available in well over 1,000 outlets, online and on home shopping channels.

These outlets range in size from tiny little corner shops to massive hypermarkets and cash and carrys. There was a completely different process for getting the products into each kind of outlet but, in essence, we had to sell our vision of trying to reinvent the world of jam to each of them.

I'd like to give you an insight into how we went about finding out who all of our potential customers were and all of the different methods we've used to convince them to buy our products. For some customers, it's been necessary to meet them in person and pitch our products to them; for others we've had to advertise in the trade press or attend trade fairs.

Of course, it's all very well convincing retailers and wholesalers to put our products onto their shelves, but we then need to find ways of encouraging consumers to pick them back off again and put them in their shopping trolleys. To do that, we have experimented with handing out samples in stores, giving away free jars with major newspapers and printing tens of millions of money-off coupons in magazines.

Afraid of Selling

I personally find selling, especially cold calling, a terrifying experience. A lot of the time, especially for a business like

SuperJam, the future of your business rests in the hands of one supermarket buyer and that puts a lot of pressure on you to impress them enough to believe in your brand. Having said that, there are a lot of things I have learned from selling door to door in the early days, from selling at a market stall as things grew, as well as more recently over the phone, and during face-to-face meetings with the biggest retailers in the world.

I think most people are quite fearful of selling; it is out of their comfort zone to call someone up and try to sell them a product, no matter how much they love the product themselves. You might be afraid of the prospect of having to call up potential customers out of the blue, or of pitching your product to the buyers of large retailers, hoping that they will give you your big break. It can definitely be scary, especially when there's so much at stake.

The prospect of people turning you down is also pretty scary. I first began knocking on doors when I was 14 and, as you can imagine, most of them would be closed in my face by people who didn't like jam, made their own jam or just didn't buy things from kids who turned up at their door. Every dozen houses or so, there'd be a sweet old lady or a smiling mum who would be more than willing to try a pot of my homemade jam.

You have to go into selling with an expectation that most people will turn you down; that is simply the reality of it. But you have to look forward to that occasional person who thinks that your product is the best thing since sliced bread. Once you get their order, that'll fire you up to keep going.

Finding Customers

Where you should look for customers will depend very much on whether you are selling to the trade or directly to the public. Selling directly to consumers could well involve advertising in the mass media, buying databases of addresses or handing out information in the streets. Finding trade buyers, on the other hand, will be an entirely different game: going to trade fairs, calling up head offices and pitching your products in person to the buyers. For most products, there are usually all kinds of different markets that you could sell through: online, to large retailers, to independent retailers, on home shopping channels, to restaurants and so on.

For every product or service, there will be a core market of companies or people that you expect to buy your products. Of course, there could well be hundreds of other smaller niches within that. In my view, there is a lot to be said for focusing on one of these markets, supermarkets for instance, and doing everything you can to become a success with them. By focusing all of your energies on understanding one group of customers and convincing them of your concept, you will have a much greater chance of success.

Depending on which kind of market you are in, you might need to find the names of only a dozen buyers. For instance, in the jam market there are only really a handful of massive retailers that you can sell your product to; if you want to build a sizeable business, that is. In other markets, such as hairdressing equipment, you might be looking to get your hands on a database of the names and phone numbers of thousands of potential customers.

You can start by finding the names, phone numbers and addresses of your potential customers in the phone book (or the online version), which is free and really easy to do. You might start by targeting all of the hairdressers' shops in Liverpool by calling them all up and asking if it would be OK for you to send them your catalogue. Then call back a couple of weeks later and ask if they want to order anything.

There are reputable companies that sell massive databases of potential customers, including the Royal Mail. You can usually buy this information for a relatively low cost. Don't be afraid to negotiate when you are buying databases from these companies; they collect the data for free from publicly available records and sell it on at a huge mark-up. So don't be afraid to offer them less than they ask for it.

You can find databases for all the fish and chip shops in Britain, all the women who've just had a baby, all the people who've just moved into a new house or all the accountancy firms with more than 50 employees, for example. Let's say you want to promote your painting and decorating company. You might buy a list of all of the people in your city who have recently moved into a new home; they're pretty likely to be wanting to do some redecorating. You might send them a box of chocolates saying: 'Welcome to the area. We're the most trusted local painter and decorator, so feel free to get in touch if you're thinking of doing any decorating.'

By only targeting the people you reckon are most likely to be interested in your services, you save yourself a lot of time and money that would be wasted if you simply tried selling to everyone.

Knowing Who You Are Selling To

What is most important to understand when you're trying to sell to someone is to know what they are looking for. Don't be afraid to ask questions and do everything you can to understand their business.

If you're targeting a supermarket buyer, what else are they selling in their stores and where could your product fit in? Which brands are performing well and which ones would they consider dropping to make space for yours? Of course, they will want to hear all about what you're going to do to make the product a success in their stores.

Usually, one of the biggest factors stopping buyers from taking on your product is the risk involved for them. If your product doesn't sell as well as what they were selling before, they'll be missing out on sales. If your brand doesn't sell at all, they will be lumbered with all the stock you've sold them.

It can be a good idea to help them get over that risk by, for example, giving them their first couple of cases of stock for free to try the product out in their stores.

You must remind yourself that the buyer is making a completely commercial decision when they choose whether or not to stock your brand: what will make their stores more money, your product or someone else's? You can't expect them to be emotional and pick you just because you're a nice guy. They'll be just as tough with you as they will with Procter & Gamble.

Consumers, on the other hand, buy products almost entirely out of emotion. So if you are selling directly to the public on your website, in your own store or at a market stall, for instance, you will do well to bear that in mind. Don't put your energy into comparing your product with the other options on the market or telling people all about its great features. Let people try it out, taste it, smell it, feel it. You want to help them imagine how it will fit into their lives. Tell them all about your story and get them caught up in your passion for the product. If you love what you're doing as much as you should, that enthusiasm will be infectious and consumers will get excited about it too.

Building a Relationship

Whether they're supermarket buyers or little old ladies on their doorsteps, people buy from other people. You could be selling the greatest thing in the world, but if they don't like you as a person you've got no chance.

The more of a relationship you can build with the people buying your products, the more likely they are to stick with you and maybe buy even more of your products. Having a relationship with someone usually means taking an interest in them, making them laugh and being someone that they enjoy doing business with.

Take the opportunity to teach them about what they can do with your products; give them tips and ideas. You can also send articles you read or things you come across to your customers, if you think they'll find them interesting.

Whether someone places an order or not, ask if it's OK for you to get back to them in one month, two months or a year, whatever is relevant for your product. Keep in touch with them, without being annoying, and try to build a relationship with them. Hopefully, if they didn't buy from you first time round, they'll remember who you are and trust you on the next occasion you get in touch; by then they could well be interested in buying from you.

Although it is great if you can build a personal relationship with all of the people buying your products, that isn't necessarily always possible. You may need to communicate with thousands, even millions, of people at once. Most likely, this will be through PR and advertising, and exactly what form that takes will depend a lot on your business.

Deciding what kind of advertising to invest in for your business can be somewhat trial and error; you might do well to try a few different forms of advertising and see which works best for you. Of course, you will want to find a way of promoting your brand at a cost that suits your budgets and in a way that reaches as many people as possible; or, that is, as many people who are in your target market as possible.

Print Advertising

Promoting your business through advertising can be expensive and it is notoriously difficult to measure how successful a campaign has been. Most people won't read your advert and your product will probably only be relevant to a few of the people who do anyway. Having said that, print advertising in a specialist magazine can be great for reaching a particular niche of the market. You might even find that you can use print advertising to sell your products directly to readers, by offering a phone number or address they can order from. Your challenge is to find places to advertise your brand where as many of the people reading or listening or watching are going to be interested in it as possible. In the case of SuperJam, advertising in women's magazines, food magazines and the Scottish press has allowed us to get our message to hundreds of thousands of our target consumers.

A well-designed advert can do a wonderful job of selling your product, but if you don't invest in creating something that looks good and gets your message across, it can end up doing more damage than good.

SuperJam hasn't invested a great deal in advertising; I much prefer putting that money into handing out samples of the products and letting people taste how great they are. Having said that, the few adverts that we have run in the national press and women's magazines have taught me a few things.

An advert should be really simple, easy to read or watch, and it shouldn't be trying to ram a product down people's throats. You wouldn't get far if you went around shouting at people 'buy my stuff!' and advertising is the same as that; you should create adverts that interest people, that they want to pay attention to and hopefully you can take the chance to get your message across. Your advert should communicate really clearly why people should buy your product. what its 'unique selling point' is. They're going to have to understand your brand in a matter of seconds and you can't afford to waste that time with information that isn't important.

Design the advert to be appropriate to its surroundings and relevant to the people who might come across it. If you're advertising in print, buy that magazine or paper for a few weeks or months and take note of which adverts appear again and again. More often than not, it will be the mail order adverts towards the back; those are the only advertisers who know for sure that what they are printing is working, because people are sending in cheques to order the products they are advertising. Usually, they are designed to look like a normal magazine article, with lots of text and good photography.

If you can print a coupon or offer a discount code alongside your advert, you'll be able to track how many people have ordered since seeing the advert. That makes it a little more measurable, and if you get hundreds of orders, you'll know that it has worked.

Giving It All Away

Using newspapers as a way to promote brands fascinates me. Done well, print advertising can really communicate a lot about your story and get people excited about your brand. It creates an opportunity to speak to millions of people in a way that isn't necessarily as aggressive as television or radio.

I once read that William Wrigley, the founder of the eponymous chewing gum empire, established himself by sending a free packet of chewing gum to everyone listed in the American phone books, 1.5 million people or so. A lot of them got in touch to buy his product at full price and the rest is history.

Partly inspired by that story, I thought it would be fun to give away SuperJam and see what happened. With the help of a marketing agency who had great connections with all of the major newspapers, we got in touch with them to ask whether they would be interested in running a promotion where we could offer all of their readers a free jar of jam. A lot of newspapers jumped at the chance, because, by offering something for free to people buying their paper, they can sell more copies.

So we went with the biggest paper of all and printed a coupon on the front page of *The Sun* newspaper offering readers a free jar of SuperJam if they took the coupon to one of our stockists. *The Sun* is the biggest selling newspaper in the English-speaking world. Something like 5.5 million people read it every day and I found myself on the front page of the Susan Boyle Special Edition of the paper— undoubtedly my proudest moment as a Scot!

Needless to say, tens of thousands of free jars were distributed and we ran out of jam that day. Sales in the weeks after the experiment took a significant step up, so I guessed that it had worked.

I repeated the offer a few more times, experimenting with all kinds of different newspapers and magazines and favouring the ones with the best response rates, eventually printing more than 50 million coupons in newspapers and women's magazines. They had a combined face value of tens of millions of pounds and so it was definitely a scary time; I was worried that one day everyone would take their coupons to the supermarkets to get free jam and we wouldn't have enough money to pay for it.

By running all of these promotions in the national press, we were able to introduce the SuperJam brand to millions of people and, since we were using coupons, we could measure how effective it was. In the end, we could see that the promotions brought with them a huge uplift in sales and the cost of running them was quickly covered.

Although this mass-media approach worked really well for SuperJam, a lot of the time you will need to discover ways of promoting your brand that are much more targeted to specific customers. You may well consider getting in touch with them by post.

Direct Mail

Although you might think it's one of the least glamorous ways of promoting your business, sending things through the post can sometimes be really effective. This isn't going to be appropriate for every kind of business, but it can work really well if you're promoting your brand in a particular area, maybe by sending them a leaflet about your newly launched service. It can also be a great way to get your message out there if your business involves selling to businesses that there are thousands of, like independent stores, hairdressers or accountancy firms.

Of course, having a leaflet show up in your letterbox can come across as pretty rude; at the end of the day, it is spam and not many people want to sit down with a cup of tea and read all of the spam that's been sent to them. So why not send something that's exciting and interesting? If you send targeted, personalized information, the chance of people reading it is a lot higher than if you just send them junk mail.

And the more targeted your direct mail campaign is, the more success you're likely to have. If you only send your materials to the people you know are likely to be interested in what you have to offer, you could find that a lot of them get in touch with you. It is possible to get the addresses of individual people by using the services of the Royal Mail and other large marketing companies. Alternatively, you can find the addresses of thousands of potential business customers by using companies that have access to Companies House records. They can provide you with the names, addresses and phone numbers of all of the businesses that describe themselves as 'hairdressers' or 'accountancy firms' in their annual return.

Like any kind of promotional activity, when you design the materials you plan on sending out, you should put a lot of thought into their look and feel. You should aim to come up with a way of getting your message across to consumers without shouting in their face.

Nowadays, people don't really write letters to one another, so a certain magic has been lost. I don't know about you, but I still find it quite exciting when something shows up at the door, such as a postcard from a friend in a country far away or a gift from a relative.

The trick with direct marketing is to try to capture some of that excitement. Why not produce a beautiful magazine about tourist destinations around the world as a way of promoting your family holiday business? If you can use the data you've acquired to send your brochure only to families who can afford the kind of holidays you are offering, your chance of success is multiplied.

One business that really captures the magic of receiving things in the post is called Matter Box. You should check it out. A friend of mine, Tim Milne, set up the company a few years ago with the vision of sending consumers who have opted in to the service a box filled with fun items from brands every month. The boxes turn up on Saturday mornings, when people have time to sit down with a cup of tea and check out all of the things they have been sent: maybe a new chocolate bar from Cadbury's, an exclusive DVD from the BBC or a bottle opener from a big beer brand.

Because time and thought has been put into creating each Matter Box, when it arrives at people's houses they really do want to open it. It is testament to the power of designing direct marketing properly, not just sticking spam through people's doors. It has been a major success and Tim has sold the idea to Royal Mail, who've now signed up over 100,000 consumers to receive the boxes.

Your direct mail might not even involve physically posting your marketing material through people's letterboxes. You could well promote your business using email marketing, perhaps with a monthly newsletter or weekly special offer. What is really exciting about email marketing is that you can design your campaign to offer an entirely personalized email for each and every one of your customers. For instance, you might know what they ordered last time they visited your site, so why not offer them something similar? You know that they opened your email two months ago when you offered a money-off code, so perhaps you should do the same again.

If you put some thought into your direct marketing, you can make it tie in really well with what you're doing online, by driving people to your website, blog and online shop.

Online Advertising

No matter what kind of business you're running, you will have to do some kind of offline promotion, by advertising or direct marketing or simply meeting people. For many businesses, advertising online can be a great opportunity.

We all know how quickly the internet is taking over from mainstream media: people read the news online, watch movies and even read books. Where people's eyeballs go, inevitably advertisers follow, making the internet one of the most likely places you might consider to promote your business, especially if you are selling online.

The wonderful thing about advertising online is that its success or failure is a great deal more measurable than most other forms of advertising. Let's say you're selling flowers and you buy a Google adword for 'Mother's Day'. Every time someone searches for Mother's Day, your link will appear at the side of the search results. If they click on your advert, you might have to pay Google 50p. If one in twenty people places an order, for the sake of argument, it will be costing you £10 to get each new customer. You might make £20 from selling them a bunch of flowers, so you're quids in.

It could make sense for you to set up an affiliate scheme, offering other websites the chance to promote your business, in exchange for a commission on any business they pass your way. Amazon and other online retailers do this really effectively and these commission incentives give someone like a blogger a great reason to write a good review of a book or feature a product they love.

You're going to need a bit of patience when you're experimenting with online advertising and be willing to try out lots of different ads: Google Adwords, banner ads, Facebook ads and maybe affiliate links. You can figure out which ones work for your business and which don't by keeping an eye on how many sales you're getting from each particular campaign.

Rather than buying ad space, you may well invest in creating a video advert or even a programme about your topic and upload it to YouTube. If it's interesting and engaging to watch, people will share it with their friends and when they search for your topic, your video will come up. You should be as creative as you can and don't be afraid to be completely off the wall.

There's a guy in America called Gary Vaynerchuck who runs a business called Wine TV. Every week, he uploads a different video of himself talking about a particular bottle of wine. He's a really eccentric character and talks about wine in a way that nobody has done before; he might describe one bottle as tasting like Twizzlers and another like sweaty socks. His videos pull in a massive audience because they're hilarious, educational and fun to watch. Although he doesn't use them as a way of giving people the hard sell on wines, his wine store does pretty well as a result of his cult following.

Video is in a lot of ways the most powerful way of telling people a story: they can see the product in action and if they see you explaining how it works in a straightforward way, they can hopefully understand why they might want to buy one. If your online videos are really popular, you may well consider running them as adverts on television.

Television Advertising

You probably imagine that television advertising is super expensive and completely out of the question as a means to promote your business. While a lot will depend on the type of business you are in and the margins that you are able to make, I don't think you should rule it out entirely. You will either need to have really wide distribution of your brand, in supermarkets or chain stores, or you will have to make it super easy for people who watch your advert to order directly from you.

As a general rule, you should expect to set aside a budget of at least £50,000 to create a simple ad campaign, with half of that money being spent on buying airtime. The response rate from your ad will depend entirely on how wide an appeal it has and how effective your advert is, but you shouldn't expect it to cost less than a pound or two to gain each new customer. If your product doesn't generate margins significantly higher than that, then advertising on television could be a quick way to waste a lot of money.

The number of smaller companies that are finding television a great way to promote their brands might surprise you. There are lots of online brands, like personalized card company Moonpig and insurance price comparison site Confused.com, that have built multimillion-pound brands almost from nothing, through advertising on television.

It is possible to create a simple advert on a relatively modest budget, perhaps by telling people about your business yourself, as the founder, if you feel confident in front of the camera. Of course, you're not likely to be able to afford advertising after *Coronation Street* or at any other peak time. It is more likely that you will have to buy airtime on a small digital channel or maybe choose to run your advert at cheaper times of day, like during the night.

You might even want to investigate running adverts on local television, if your business is focused on a particular area. There are often discounts available for first-time advertisers, so be sure to ask for them. Whatever way you consider advertising on television, make sure that you research thoroughly and take as much advice as you can. Organisations like Thinkbox, which is in charge of promoting television advertising on behalf of commercial broadcasters, can offer a lot of support and advice for first-time advertisers.

Television advertising is undoubtedly the most glamorous form of getting your name out there, but you must be absolutely sure that it's right for your business. You might even find that there are opportunities to sell your product on television without having to pay for airtime by, for instance, selling your products on home shopping channels.

SuperJam in the Spotlight

One place I had never really imagined I would find myself was in the studio of the leading home shopping channel in the world, QVC. Home shopping in the UK is a massive, often forgotten and misunderstood market, but billions of pounds a year are spent by people watching home shopping channels.

There is a perception that channels like QVC give viewers the hard sell on stuff that they don't really need. In fact, since they offer a 100% money-back guarantee, that isn't really the case. Anything bought from them can be sent back for a full refund if, for whatever reason, the person who ordered it changes their mind.

Because of this, they're always looking for products that are of great quality and that they can offer at a price that beats anyone else in the market. A shopper who gets a great deal is unlikely to send their order back.

QVC has a particular interest in quality brands with great stories behind them, so SuperJam seemed like a great fit. It invited me onto one of its shows to tell its viewers my story and offer a selection of our jams, a cookbook and an tote at a special price. The producers of the show were really excited about my visit; I was the youngest ever guest on QVC!

After an audition to find out if I was going to be able to tell my story on camera, we had our first trial on QVC at 3 p.m. one night in April 2011, at a time when things were really taking off for SuperJam.

The show lasted around ten minutes, although it flew by for me, and there was a lot at stake. The bar is set pretty high for any new product launching on QVC. Its minimum expectation for sales is over hundreds of pounds for every minute you are on air, so I really wasn't sure if we would sell enough.

Thankfully, the phone lines were red hot and we took hundreds of orders in a matter of minutes. Everyone was delighted with how the show went and I was invited back to do it all over again.

QVC has since become one of our biggest customers and we are talking about offering our products to its viewers in other countries; hopefully one day on QVC in America. This shows that you can find a market for your products in places that aren't immediately obvious. In fact, you might find that the best way of marketing your business isn't necessarily advertising at all—money might well be better spent on getting out there and meeting potential customers in person.

Events and Trade Fairs

One of the best ways we've found for meeting new stockists and promoting the brand to consumers has been big events like trade shows, music festivals and food fairs. You might well find out about an event that you feel would be ideal for your brand and decide to set up a stall there, showing your brand off to the possibly thousands of people who come along. You can take the opportunity to hand out samples and promotional materials and maybe collect people's contact details by offering a prize draw.

I've found that having something exciting going on at your installation or booth at a show can draw hundreds of people towards your brand. It's a great opportunity to meet potential customers face to face and tell them all about your story. You should make an effort to collect people's business cards or contact details, so that you can follow up with a phone call or a meeting to hopefully win their business. If they remember meeting you at the event, chances are they'll be happier to talk to you than if you were just someone calling up out of the blue.

Usually we take our 1973 VW camper van, Valerie, to these events. I call her the 'Jam Mobile'. She doesn't go very fast and has been known to break down at the worst possible moment, but people love coming over to check out what we're doing. That's usually handing out scones and jam and signing copies of the cookbook.

Attending events and trade fairs is a great way of meeting other entrepreneurs and companies that are operating in a similar field to you. You can talk shop with them, find out where they sell their products and who you should be speaking to as well. You might even discover that you can form partnerships with other companies to help one another find new customers.

Partnerships with Other Brands

One of the great things about jam is that it's pretty versatile: you can eat it on porridge or toast for breakfast, on a scone for afternoon tea or make yourself a humble jam sandwich for lunch. Not to mention all of the things that you can bake with it.

All of these different uses for jam have opened up a whole world of possibilities for collaborating and working with other brands. We've done some really fun things with a quirky tea company called Today Was Fun, with Rodda's

Cornish Clotted Cream, Feel Good Drinks and even with an oatcake company called Nairn's.

By working with these complementary companies, we can share the cost of promotions and help each other with introductions to one another's customers.

One of the most successful partnerships has been with Rodda's; jam tastes great on a scone with clotted cream, the classic afternoon tea treat. Working together, we have employed a team of people who are passionate about SuperJam to hand out cream teas in supermarket stores. By sharing the cost of the promotion, we have been able to promote both products side by side and both companies have prospered from it.

You will no doubt be able to find all sorts of companies that you can work with to promote your brand. Perhaps there will be complementary products that people might buy to use alongside yours or maybe you'll just want to work with some companies that share your ethos.

Whether you work in partnership with another brand to sell your products or whether you go it alone, you'll find that there are all sorts of opportunities to get your brand out there for you to explore. Don't be afraid to try out all the different kinds of advertising and, most importantly, don't be frightened of picking up the phone or going out and meeting people, telling people about your story. If you want your business to grow, you're going to have to sell.

Making Your Sales Go Viral: Groupon (groupon.com)

You might well have come across Groupon, since it's been something of an internet sensation over the past year or so. It's apparently the fastest company in history to go from starting up to being worth over a billion dollars. All from the power of people recommending great deals to their friends.

What has made Groupon grow at this lightning pace has been its use of social media. The concept for the site is fairly simple: it signs up a business that wants to promote its product or service at a heavily discounted price to try to reel in hundreds of new customers. The benefit to the business of promoting itself on Groupon is that, hopefully, the customers will come back again and pay full price, and maybe even recommend the brand to their friends.

There is a maximum number of people who are allowed to get the deal, which creates a sense of 'quick, buy now before they're all gone!' The clever twist is that the deal is only activated if a minimum number of consumers sign up for it, maybe 500 or 1,000 people. Because everyone is so desperate to get the deal, they tell all their friends about it and encourage them to sign up too, making the whole thing go viral.

There are now hundreds of these so-called 'group buying' sites, offering a different deal each day for particular cities. They make money by taking a cut of the value of the voucher that people buy for the business that is being promoted; it might be a £100 voucher for a top restaurant that is being sold on Groupon for only £30, and Groupon takes maybe 50% of that.

The success of these kinds of businesses shows the power of making it really easy for people to recommend your brand to their friends on Twitter, Facebook and other social media. If you can harness some of that power to help sell your products, you'll be on to a winner!

8 Love Your Customers

There are very few businesses in the world that truly put their customer at the heart of everything they do. Some companies can seem distracted by the opinions of shareholders, managers and people other than the customer, whose intentions tend not be in the customers' best interests.

And there aren't a lot of businesses that start every day by thinking about how they can do what they do even better to make their customers happier. Usually, they try to figure out how to make more money in the short term, how to cut costs and how to make their own lives easier.

Sometimes, though, a company comes along that really sees itself through the customers' eyes. It understands that if it makes the customer happy, money and all that stuff will simply take care of itself.

Businesses like Virgin, FedEx and Wal-Mart have a very clear idea of what it is that their customer wants, whether that's great customer service, delivering packages on time or cheap prices. They devote their every waking moment to delivering that one simple aim consistently, and their customers love them for it.

Companies that put the customer at the heart of their business are bound to be successful, loved and profitable. For SuperJam, trying to listen to our customers and engage with them is something that I have taken really seriously. Even now, I spend a lot of my time answering calls from the people who buy our products and asking people in the supermarket store what they think when they taste our jam.

I know that this enthusiasm for talking to the people who buy our products is what has helped to make SuperJam such a success. In your business, it is going to be important that you nurture a relationship with the people who regularly buy from you and that you take every opportunity to ask what they think.

Encouraging Loyalty

All too often, we focus all of our energies on getting new customers. You go out there and call people up out of the blue and try to sell them your products. This is great, as long as it isn't taking your attention away from doing the best job you can for your everyday customers. Without the people who are already buying your products, you're finished.

There's a saying that it costs five times as much to get a new customer as it does to keep an old one, and there's definitely some truth in that. You should do everything you can to keep your existing customers on board; they are the bedrock of your business and you need them to keep placing their orders.

In essence, you want to show your regular customers that you value their business and you want to offer them a reason to keep coming back. Could you encourage them to use your products more frequently? Or maybe you can offer them an upgrade to a premium version. Your existing customer base is the most fertile place for you to look for sales, so you should make sure that you are always offering something new.

I also think that there's a lot to be said for rewarding your most loyal customers. Take every opportunity you can to say thank you and let them know that you really value their business. Why not send them a personal letter to say thanks and maybe enclose a token of your appreciation, a bottle of champagne or a box of chocolates, for instance.

You could even consider setting up a loyalty programme that offers rewards to the customers who spend the most with you. This could be as simple as having a card that you stamp every time the customer visits your store and giving them a freebie once they've collected a certain number of stamps.

Perhaps the most powerful loyalty scheme in the world is the Tesco Clubcard. By taking note of everything you buy from its stores, Tesco can build up a profile of what type of person you are. Maybe you're a young family that eats only organic food, for example. It can then send you offers for organic products that it thinks you might be likely to buy. If, for example, it sees that you don't buy any milk from its stores, it can assume that you buy it somewhere else and send you some money-off vouchers for organic milk, to encourage you to start buying it from Tesco.

The more you understand about your customers, the better you can encourage them to become loyal to you. Perhaps you know when their birthday is. You can offer them a free meal at your restaurant on their birthday—of course, they're not likely to come on their own and they might even bring a whole party with them. If this kind of thing is done well, it could be a really touching way of saying thank you, but also probably a pretty smart business decision too.

Don't be afraid of saying thank you to the people who keep you in business; show them you understand who they are and that you love them.

Talk to Your Customers

The best way to show your customers that you value them is to listen to what they have to say. Tell them in person how grateful you are for their business and always ask what you can do to improve things for them. By requesting their feedback, you can find ways of making your products even better, and perhaps your existing customers will give you ideas for how to find new ones. What do they think you do really well and where do they feel you let them down? Maybe they think you don't shout enough about the things they love you for. Or perhaps there's something that they feel isn't up to scratch.

The best way to get a perspective on how the customer experiences your product or service is to put yourself in their shoes and experience it yourself. Perhaps you could send a mystery shopper into your store or actually browse your own website and place an order. You need to imagine what they will think when they look at your product: do the labels look cheap or is the floor dirty?

Don't forget your front-line employees either, who are in a prime position to understand what kind of experience your customers are having. They are the only people in your business who really know how the customer feels. Talk openly with them about what the customers think you need to improve and have somewhere for them to make a note of complaints and compliments alike.

Your employees don't enjoy hearing complaints from customers every day, so foster a culture where if a customer makes a complaint to you, it is your responsibility to find a solution so that nobody ever has the same complaint again. In a company where the customer is saying great things about your brand and telling your employees how much they love it, they will be so much more motivated in their job. They will really believe that what they are offering is a worthwhile product that they can believe in.

And of course, there's nothing like hearing from your customers what they think—so ask them! Give them a comment card with a stamp and address on it along with their delivery and encourage them to tell you what they think. Maybe enter them into a competition if they send the card back. Try to keep it simple, by just asking one question like 'How could we make our service even better?' or 'What do you love about us?'

Opening up a conversation with your customers is now a lot easier than before, with new technologies like social networks and blogs providing a means to connect with them. If you are successful in creating an online community, by getting people to become fans of your brand on Facebook for instance, that gives you a great opportunity to talk to the people buying your product. Why not ask them for ideas, comments and suggestions? You can even make it into a competition where the best idea wins some freebies.

Why not have a bit of fun with it and invite your customers round for beer and pizza or a cup of coffee, whatever is appropriate, and pick their brains. The customers who love you will be more than willing to spend their time helping you to improve your business. And the ones who don't will love having a platform to vent their frustrations about what they think you need to change.

The Lovers and the Haters

There are two groups of people that a business should be really keen to hear from:

1. The people who love you.
2. The people who hate you.

Every business has customers who love them and it feels great when they get in touch to say so. They're the ones who call you up to say how much they enjoy your service, who tell all their friends about you and come back again and again. If you take the time to ask them *why* they love you, you'll find that they're more than happy to talk to you and tell you anything you want to know. They'll help you to understand the essence of your brand, what it is that actually makes people buy your product, why they love it and why they come back for more.

You might even find that their reasons for loving you are different from what you imagine your brand is all about, which can be really surprising and useful to know. For instance, perhaps you've been shouting about how cheap your prices are, while all along the reason people like you is that your location is really convenient, or your service is faster than anywhere else. If they like you enough, they'll probably even offer you some good ideas and give up their time to help you improve your service.

Then there are the people who hate you. Hate is probably too strong a word, but you know what I mean: the people who don't think you've done your job properly. The angry people who phone you up with a complaint that you don't want to hear about. You might think that their complaint is ridiculous, but that doesn't matter. Someone who paid their hard-earned money for your service isn't happy about it, and if you take the time to find out why, you have the opportunity to make a change. Most companies take the people who love their brand for granted and try to get the people who complain off the phone as fast as possible. If you take it as a chance to improve your business, you might just be able to turn those angry people into people who love your business instead.

Acting on Feedback

It's all very well collecting all of these comments, but they don't have any value unless you take the time to listen to what your customers have to say and try to do something about it. You might find that you don't agree with their views or you might even find what they say offensive. Whatever they write, you have to take it on board and use it to improve your business. Try out the ideas they suggest to you and do your best to fix the problems they tell you about.

You must be willing to change your products, your pricing or even your entire business model, based on the feedback that your customers give you. They are the people you need to impress and if they tell you what they want, this is exactly what you should be doing. Of course, some people will make suggestions that aren't practical and a lot of complaints will be the result of a one-off mistake. You have to focus your energies on solving the problems that people repeatedly tell you about and launching the products that are requested most often.

It is inevitable that, unfortunately, there will be occasions when something goes really wrong. Perhaps one of your employees is rude to a customer, or a delivery turns up broken or you don't deliver on what you promised for whatever reason. You will, once in a while, find yourself with a big complaint on your hands, and how you deal with it will be a test of your commitment to making your customers happy.

When something goes wrong, always make the effort to call or meet with the customer and explain in an honest and open way that you screwed up. Apologize as sincerely as you can and in a way that they can empathize with; don't merely send a standard letter with a money-off coupon attached. Really show them that you care and that you feel bad about what has happened; ask what you can do to make things better. Usually, a sincere apology in itself is enough to show that what has happened isn't an everyday event. Be generous with replacement products and refunds.

Thankfully, SuperJam hasn't had too many things that have gone terribly wrong. Of course, there has been the occasional jar of jam that has been opened in a supermarket or smashed in the post on its way to a customer's home. We always send an overwhelming amount of free jam to people who have experienced something going wrong and, as it happens, some of the nicest letters I have ever received have been from those people writing back to say thank you.

Perhaps when something has gone wrong it is going to prompt you to have a think about how you can change the way you do things to stop it happening again. Why not invite the person who complained into your company premises to tell you how they think you should be running things? You never know, they might just give you some good ideas.

Replying to Every Letter

For SuperJam, trying to listen to every comment, every criticism, every idea that customers have, has been a major focus for me.

It has always been a principle of mine that every single letter that someone sends to us, whether they're just writing to say how much they love SuperJam or writing to complain that they feel we're overpriced, gets a reply. Not only with a standard letter but with one that someone from the company has taken the time to write out thoughtfully and in a friendly way.

In the early days, if someone called the number on the back of a jar of SuperJam, which was an official-looking number, their call would come straight to my mobile phone. As you can imagine, most people calling up were very surprised to be speaking with the owner of the company!

That set-up came about mainly because I was the only person in the company at the time, so there wasn't anyone else to answer the phone. But what I realized was that having direct contact with the people who were buying our products was hugely powerful. Even though I now have a team of people who help out answering the phone and replying to letters, I still answer a lot of phone calls myself. From people who merely want to ask where their local store is or those who want to know why we don't make chutney, I think it's crucial to pay attention to what people are getting in touch to say, no matter how senior you are in your company.

Much of the time, people won't be complaining to you about massive issues. You'd be amazed at how annoyed people can get at what, to you, might seem trivial. You're going to need to listen to all of these tiny little things that people find annoying about your business—the font on your menu is too small, the chairs screech on the floor or whatever it might be—and make dozens of small changes to improve your product. A good example of this for SuperJam was that in the early days we had a lot of people complaining that the labels were difficult to take off. For people who wanted to be green and reuse their jam jars, that was a problem. It seemed like the most trivial issue but it attracted a lot of complaints. So, as you would expect, we changed the labels and that became one of many tiny changes we've made over time to continually improve our packaging, our recipes and our marketing.

If we had simply ignored those complaints, we wouldn't have made that easy change to our product that turned people from complaining about it to loving it. By listening to all of the silly little complaints, the big ideas and the wacky suggestions that our customers make, we improve our products and our marketing all the time. I love hearing feedback and maintaining a conversation with the people who love our brand.

Creating a Sense of Community

As the business took off, I found that we were being inundated with letters, emails and phone calls from people who loved the brand. They really liked it that someone had brought out a healthier kind of jam and appreciated the charity work, and loads of people had ideas for new directions in which we could take the business.

Historically, it wasn't possible for a grocery brand, like SuperJam, to nurture a meaningful connection with the people buying its products. There was always someone in between, like a retailer, making it hard for the brand to have much contact with the consumer. But now, by having a website and perhaps a presence on social networks, it is possible to connect with the people buying your products. They can learn more about your story, your business and your ethos, and hopefully you can understand more about who they are and what they want.

It sounds pretty simple, but I love the idea that when something happens at SuperJam, everyone who cares about the brand knows about it right away. From people who put SuperJam on their toast every morning, those who work on the production line, supermarket buyers and everyone who volunteers at the tea parties, they can all find out in an instant when we launch a new product, or share with us the exciting news that a new supermarket has taken us on.

The online world in particular has made it possible to have a meaningful dialogue with the 10,000 or so people who really care about SuperJam. It has created, I suppose, a sense of community. By having a blog, a Facebook page, Twitter and all the rest of it, we were able to start having more of a conversation with these people who loved SuperJam and wanted to see it succeed. We can invite them to comment on what we're doing, ask for suggestions of where to take the business and really just provide a platform for them to tell us what they think.

One of the best ways in which we have used social media is by having a 'suggest a store' page on our website, which we promote on the blog, Twitter and everywhere else.

We encourage our fans to tell us about a shop in their area that they think should sell SuperJam. That might be an upmarket deli, an earthy farm shop or just their local grocery store.

We then send out a postcard to the suggested shop, letting them know that one of their customers thinks they should stock SuperJam, with some information about the products and an introductory offer for the store. If the outlet places an order, we send out a free jar of jam to the person who made the suggestion.

It's a really simple idea, but it's worked really well. Thousands of people have suggested stores to us and, since they are shops that they know and like, a lot of them have placed an order and it has helped us to get the brand into hundreds of independent stores.

I also love having an email newsletter, which goes out to tens of thousands of people who have signed up to receive it. It gives us a chance to update them on what's going on at the company and I like using it to pose questions to our fans: what should be the next flavour we launch, or what should we do at our summer tea parties? Hundreds of people will reply to the newsletter right away with their suggestions.

The conversation with your customers can be like an open tap, with an almost limitless flow of ideas, suggestions and information coming from them to you. In a sense, it turns conventional marketing on its head: it used to be about companies feeding information about their products to customers, but now the people who love your brand can talk back and tell you how they think you should be doing things.

However you communicate with your customers—by text message, blogging, letters, noticeboards, or whatever—what is important is that you engage with them. Make the effort to understand what they want and how you can do what you do even better for them.

Doing so makes it possible for all of the people who care about your business to be kept up to date regularly, with everything going on at the company. SuperJam gives customers a chance to be involved with thinking up ideas for new products, assisting with organizing tea parties in their area and helping the company to grow.

You could say that this has created a feeling that we're all in it together, as a group of people who believe in something—whether that's the idea of making jam healthier, the idea of doing business in a different way, challenging the status quo in an industry that has been around for hundreds of years or simply the idea of putting a smile on the faces of thousands of lonely elderly people.

Whether it has been through social media or merely taking the time to read the letters that our customers send in, SuperJam has been able to learn what people think we're doing a great job of and what they consider we should improve. We have opened ourselves up to the idea of having a conversation with the people buying our products and as the years go by, we'll get to know them even better. The more we know about the people who put SuperJam on their toast, the more we can improve our products, our marketing and our outlets and, hopefully, they'll love us in return for it.

A Customer Service Company that Happens to Be in the Business of Selling Shoes: Zappos (zappos.com)

I had the pleasure of meeting Tony Hsieh, the founder of Zappos.com, in California a couple of years ago, not long before Amazon acquired his business for over a billion dollars. His is a business that turns a lot of business conventions on their head and, for me, has been a big inspiration.

A few years ago, it would have seemed like a fantasy that you could make a business out of selling shoes over the internet. Surely people want to try shoes on before buying them? Well, Zappos lets them do just that—with free next-day shipping and returns. Its call centre employees offer legendary customer service and because of that, they have built a $1 billion company selling shoes online.

Zappos puts a huge amount of emphasis on the importance of its company culture and the impact it has on the service its customers receive. As an example, when a new member of staff joins the team and goes through their two-week training, they are offered $3,000 to leave the company. Very few people take up the offer, even though it's a huge amount of money, because they're so keen to work for Zappos. Tony figures that the ones who leave probably wouldn't have been a good fit for the company.

His is a company that understands the importance of creating a great culture and is focused on wanting to make its customers happy.

9 Do Good

I am sure that for you, starting a business is not all about making money. Of course you want to make a livelihood and support your family and starting a business can definitely help do that. Who am I kidding? Starting a business might just make you a millionaire. But I know for sure that starting a business doesn't only appeal to you simply because of that.

I don't see my business as a money-making machine; I see it as the most powerful way in which I can make an impact on the world. I often imagine myself getting to the end of my life, hopefully as an old man, looking back at everything I have done. I want to feel proud. Proud of what I have created, of the decisions I've made and, most importantly, of the impact I've had on the people I've been lucky enough to share my life with. Setting up a company is exciting because of the lifestyle, the opportunity to do what you love and the chance to do good in your community. I'm sure you can imagine how much fun it will be, how much of an adventure you're going to have. There's something immensely satisfying about turning your ideas into a reality and creating something worthwhile, something that touches people's lives.

Your Chance to Change the World

So, how are you going to change the world? This probably sounds daunting and you might not have thought that starting your business could have such a big impact. Well, whether you've set out to or not, simply by setting up your business you're going to do a huge amount of good. Probably the biggest impact you will have is going to be by creating a product that people enjoy; if you put a smile on the faces of hundreds of customers every week, that has to be a good thing, right?

Businesses and entrepreneurs are the most powerful force in the world. I know that sounds like a bold thing to say, but I really believe it. If I thought that I could have a bigger impact on the world by doing something other than starting my own company, I'd be doing it.

Entrepreneurs have always been at the root of all human progress. They came up with all of the little ideas and innovations that collectively we call civilization. Without the tinkerers and traders, risk takers and marketers, inventors and garden shed eccentrics, there would be nothing. No television, no cars, no light bulbs, no jobs, no taxes, no education, no healthcare, no government—nothing.

In the modern age, entrepreneurs are the only people who can change the world. It will be entrepreneurs who solve our environmental problems. Entrepreneurs will feed the poor and liberate the populations of countries that aren't free. They'll find a way to make live-saving drugs available to people who can't afford them and, by them making the world a smaller place through technology and free media, we'll hopefully one day live on a much more peaceful planet.

Almost certainly, one of the proudest moments on your entrepreneurial journey will be the day you take on your first employee. You might be giving them their first job or taking them out of unemployment to come and work with you. You're giving them an income to support their family with and a purpose, a reason to get up in the mornings. Employing people does a huge amount of good; it literally changes people's lives.

Every time you make a sale, you'll be paying tax in one way or another. Taxes pay for schools, hospitals and aid to people in the developing world. You're making a contribution to society, and the more successful your business is, the bigger that contribution will be. Although I wouldn't try to pretend that I love writing a big fat cheque to the government at the end of the year, I do feel a sense of pride when I imagine what that money could be paying for. It is wealth that I have created that otherwise the government wouldn't have had and society would have gone without.

Small businesses are by far the biggest employers in the world, creating almost all new jobs and the lion's share of all of the wealth and taxes in society. It isn't big businesses that make the world go around, it's small ones run by entrepreneurs like you and me.

The Business of Doing Good

You're probably thinking, 'That's all well and good, but what about sweatshops and exploitation, scam artists and entrepreneurs who sell junk food to kids?' You'd be right to point out that not all entrepreneurs set out wanting to do good. Some merely see an opportunity to make a fast buck by selling stolen goods or scamming someone vulnerable.

In reality, entrepreneurs are just people; some people have good intentions and some of them don't. The businesses they start are a reflection of their values, their priorities and their interpretation of fairness. I'm sure that you will be one of the entrepreneurs who start a business with the right intentions.

You'll be in good company. Some of the most amazing business success stories from throughout history are those of the entrepreneurs who started companies not with an aim to get rich, but with an aim to make the world a better place.

Hundreds of years ago, companies were started by people like the Quakers, who had aims of improving the lives of those in their community. Since they served their customers and employees with integrity, they were very well-trusted organizations, at a time when crime and dishonesty were rife.

The companies founded by the Quakers and other similar entrepreneurs became vastly successful because of their long-term thinking. The likes of Cadbury's chocolate, Clark's shoes and Barclays bank are still household names today, hundreds of years after they were founded.

When a company is trusted, respected and people know that it is based on morally sound principles, it tends to be loved by its people, its suppliers and, most importantly, its customers.

Business as Protest

In the modern age, companies such as The Body Shop, Patagonia, Ben and Jerry's and Innocent drinks have become hugely successful by voicing strong ethical values on particular issues. This strong moral grounding is the reason they are loved by the people who work for them and everyone who buys their products. At times, they have used their marketing materials, their packaging and their reputation to protest against issues in society that they feel passionate about.

I've mentioned a number of entrepreneurs throughout this book who have been an inspiration. The late Anita Roddick, who started The Body Shop, has been a hero to me. In its early days, The Body Shop's adverts spoke more about political issues than they did about its products. They would champion women's rights, protest against animal testing and raise awareness of exploitation in the third world. In a way that almost nobody else has, Roddick showed that it is possible to build a hugely successful business while remaining true to your values. By using the business as a platform for protest and as a mouthpiece for a movement, The Body Shop continues to make consumers aware of the terrible practices of an entire industry.

Ben & Jerry's

Another business that I think has been a leading light in the world of ethical business is Ben & Jerry's. Started by two friends, not surprisingly named Ben and Jerry, in Vermont in 1978, it has grown into a massive business. Along the way, it has protested about the amount the US government spends on war with stickers on the lids of its ice cream, showing a pie chart of how that dwarves spending on education and healthcare. It has also championed the cause of gay marriage with a special 'Hubby-Hubby' flavour.

One of the most inspiring things the company has done has been to source ingredients from social enterprises, like the Grayston bakery. Started by a 'Jewish-buddhist-former-nuclear-physicist-monk' called Bernie Glassman, the bakery employs those who are economically disenfranchised. They are people who otherwise wouldn't have a lot of hope finding a job and making a life for themselves.

Ben & Jerry's also sources Brazil nuts from a company called Community Products Inc, which buys Brazil nuts from the indigenous communities of the Amazon rainforest. The idea behind this is to create an economic reason for the rainforest to exist, to make it harder for loggers to move in and destroy it for ever.

By sourcing ingredients from companies like this, Ben & Jerry's has contributed to making a lot of people's lives better. The political messages it prints on the lids of its products don't have anything to do with ice cream but, by reaching millions of people and causing a bit of a stir, it might just help to make a change.

Selling out

Ben and Jerry's was bought by the publicly listed Anglo-Dutch conglomerate Unilever in 2000. Other ethical businesses have taken this route too, with The Body Shop being taken over by cosmetics company L'Oréal and Innocent majority owned by Coca-Cola. You might say that companies like this are sell-outs, because they are now a part of the very companies that they set out to campaign against.

I actually think it is fantastic news that all of these companies have become hugely more commercially successful on an international level. The bigger and more profitable they are, the more good they can do.

They have proven that ethical business isn't a harebrained idea dreamed up by a bunch of hippies. It is now taken seriously by Wall Street and is a movement that employs millions of people. It is quite feasible for your business to grow and grow, while maintaining its values and standing up for what you believe in at the same time. One day, you could become part of a bigger company or your shares could be publicly traded.

Being part of a larger company makes it a lot easier for these ethical businesses to grow their brands around the world, taking advantage of the connections of the company that bought them. They can also become vastly more competitive by making gains from the buying power and efficiency of being part of a larger organization.

Ethical business makes good commercial sense: people want to buy products that are ethically produced, they want to work for and invest in businesses that treat people fairly and, in the long run, nobody is going to make much money if we destroy the environment.

Three Bottom Lines

Values-led companies, like the ones I have been writing about, measure their success using more yardsticks than simply profits. Some of them refer to having 'three bottom lines'—profit, community and environmental sustainability, and making an impact on their people. They take each as seriously as the others and recognize that, in the long run, their consumers will reward them for these values.

I feel as though most businesses operate as if they are in a war zone. They try to squeeze their suppliers and rip off their customers, treating their employees badly along the way. This is not a happy picture, not a way to create anything worthwhile or meaningful.

Business should be love. Love for what it is you are trying to achieve, love for your customers and your people, and love for your suppliers. You might think this sounds ridiculous, but imagine if you ripped people off on a daily basis, lied and cheated, cut corners and didn't treat the people around you fairly—you wouldn't get very far at all. You'd soon have no friends and maybe even worse.

In business you should be fair to everyone around you and enter into relationships with suppliers, customers and employees in the expectation that they will last for years. You should be honest with your customers about the benefits of your products; don't exaggerate or lie about them because, sooner or later, you'll get caught out. Don't squeeze your suppliers for every last penny because, when things are tough for you, they won't have much sympathy. Most importantly, treat your employees with respect, because without their support and loyalty, you're toast.

If you create a company that is an enjoyable and a fair place to work, that supports its local community and goes about business in an ethical way, there's a fair chance that customers and healthy profits will follow.

Profits

In a traditional company, making money is the only goal. In fact, it is a legal requirement of a publicly listed company to have maximizing profit as its priority; it is a machine that has to deliver as much of a return to its shareholders as possible. In the eyes of the system, if a company spent its energy on doing something else, it would be doing its investors a disservice.

Big companies aren't human, although they're run by people. They don't have feelings or morals and only the law can tell them what is right or wrong. In countries where they can, companies sell cigarettes to children, cause unimaginable environmental destruction and, given half the chance, bribe and corrupt governments.

There isn't such a thing as 'enough' for a public company. They have a hunger for growth that drives the capitalist machine, that lobbies for cheaper and cheaper prices, less and less regulation and more and more freedom to mistreat people, animals and the environment.

JD Rockefeller, an American oil tycoon and one of the wealthiest men in all history, famously described what he wanted from the ideal employee: 'He must be able to glide over every moral restraint with almost childlike disregard and has, amongst other positive qualities, no scruples whatsoever and be willing to kill of thousands of victims—without a murmur.'

Despite all of this, I don't think that making money is a bad thing. I'd be deluded if I thought there was a better way to motivate people to come up with ideas, create jobs and improve our lives than giving them a chance to make a buck. But what is bad is when companies want to make money at the cost of everything else, with no regard for what is right and wrong.

I think that it is possible to run a profitable company and maintain your values, stand up for what you believe in and treat people ethically.

Community and Environmental Sustainability

Independent companies, owned by entrepreneurs, are far more human. They are free to spend their energies and profits on what they like: protesting, supporting charities, employing disenfranchised youth or buying their ingredients from ethical sources.

Perhaps when you are setting your commercial goals for your business, you should also think about how you would like to make an impact on the world. What issues do you feel strongly about in society? What is great is that this can be personal to you and doesn't have to have anything to do with what you're selling. If an ice-cream company can protest about war, you can make a noise about whatever you feel strongly about too.

Set yourself a goal, ideally one that can be measured. Perhaps you want to raise £10,000 for a charity that is close to your heart, or cut the amount of waste you send to land-fill by half. When you have a goal to focus on, it makes it so much easier to do good; otherwise your efforts tend to get a bit wishy-washy.

By measuring your success in this way, using more measurements than profit alone, everything becomes a great deal more satisfying. You can see the impact you're having on your community through the smiles on people's faces or the letters of thanks you receive, and that definitely feels just as much like success as money in the bank.

What I think is starting to happen is that the movement of ethical businesses who are embracing this way of thinking is transforming the conventions of business. Some of them are being listed on the stock market and being bought by publicly listed companies, hopefully changing the whole game. It is becoming possible for a company that isn't just motivated by making money still to be hugely profitable and to grow into a well-loved, international brand.

Impact on People

Great people are attracted to work for ethical companies because they want to be part of something that is about more than money. Being part of a company that has meaning gives people a sense of pride and motivates them to work hard at making the company a success.

When you take someone on to work with you, you're inviting them to take part in your journey. It might not be clear what lies ahead or what opportunities are going to pop up along the way. You're going to have to be sure that everyone working with you understands your ambitions, but more importantly that you understand theirs.

How can you help the people working with you to achieve their dreams and ambitions for their own career? You should help them to gain the skills and experience they need to get to where they are trying to go. Their own dream might be to set up a company of their own, or to move on to work somewhere else; you simply have to embrace this.

If you offer the people in your business the chance to develop and grow, to travel, learn new things and express themselves, they will be as motivated as you are. Hopefully, you can help them to feel that they too are doing what they were born to do!

For me, starting my company is not the most important thing in my life; my family, friends and the impact that I can have on society are all far more meaningful for me. And I think that those are values that are shared by most people, but maybe even more so by people of my generation and the type of people who work at SuperJam.

Nobody wants to work for a company that is unscrupulous or immoral or that makes other people's lives miserable.

The companies that will prosper are those that embrace this; they will be moral, treat their employees fairly and place an emphasis on the importance of doing good.

I run SuperJam with the aim of building a company that challenges the status quo of an industry that has been around for hundreds of years. I get a kick from reinventing a product and creating something that hundreds of thousands of people enjoy and appreciate on their toast every morning.

Setting up a company is more about the adventure and the challenge than about trying to make heaps of money. Building something beautiful and taking pride from what you have created is what it's about for me.

I guess you need to imagine yourself on your deathbed looking back at everything you've done in life. Will you feel proud of it? Will you feel like you really did everything you wanted to do, that you gave it your best shot?

Nobody gets to their deathbed and wishes they spent more time in the office. It is important to keep everything in perspective; your business should never be the most important thing in your life. And making money definitely shouldn't be your top priority.

Often people ask me: 'How do you motivate yourself to stick at it?' The only way you can get motivated about doing anything in life is if you feel in your gut that it is right. You have to feel that it is the right thing to be doing with your life, that you are doing what you were born to do.

A Cup of Tea and a Laugh

Of course, even though making money isn't what motivates me, SuperJam is a successful company that I run in a very commercially minded way. What's exciting for me is that, with no investors or anyone else above me, I am free to invest the profits from the company in whatever way I like.

For me, the most satisfying way to spend the profits is on charitable causes that are close to my heart.

When my grandmother originally made jam, she would make jam, scones and cakes and take them with her on visits to all of the lonely elderly people in her area. These were people who were living alone or in care homes. Nobody else visited them very much and, in some ways, nobody else cared about them.

It was something that my gran felt, and still does feel, very strongly about and every time we went to see her, she would drag my brother and I with her to visit the elderly people. While she made lunch for them, my brother would play his guitar and I would tell them stories of how I wanted to set up my own business one day. One particular lady, Mary, would joke that I was going to get into 'monkey business', having forgotten she had made the same joke every time we had visited her over the years.

As kids we didn't really understand the boredom that these people faced and couldn't quite appreciate why they would cry when we left. Although we were pretty young, we knew there was something sad about them having the exact same conversation with us every time we visited, since they could barely remember anything for longer than a few minutes. As I got older, it became something that I, too, felt strongly about and as the business took off, I felt I was in a position to do something about it.

By no means was I going to come up with the solution to this massive problem; the highest rate of suicide is among women over the age of 70 and more than a million elderly people in the UK spend Christmas Day on their own. Nevertheless, I wanted to do something about the problem of elderly people being lonely.

I began by speaking with local councillors and community groups and it became clear that the biggest thing lacking in many elderly people's lives was the opportunity to socialize out of their own house or care home.

In April 2007, we started running tea parties in local community halls in my home town of Edinburgh. We would have live music, dancing, pots of tea and, of course, scones and SuperJam. It was a very simple concept but it quickly flourished. A year later, we had run over 100 events in Scotland, England and Wales, with the biggest events attracting over 500 guests!

Many the guests wanted to contribute to the project, by bringing along home baking or knitting tea cosies for the teapots. Soon we were having tea cosies sent in from all over the country and we began featuring them on our website. We have a 'Tea Cosy of the Week' competition, where the winner is sent a few cases of jam. Over time, the cosies have become more and more elaborate and creative— some are in the shape of people, animals or fruits.

Knitting has become one of the main activities of the SuperJam Tea Parties and, a few months after setting up the project, we ran a massive nationwide 'knitathon'. Guests at 100 or so subsequent tea parties were asked to knit squares. These were then sewn together to make more than 100 blankets for disabled Indian orphans.

SuperJam Tea Parties is a project that I am really ambitious about. Even though we now run events nationwide and thousands of elderly people come along, I still want it to become bigger and better over the coming years.

I'm spurred on to grow the project by the feedback from the elderly guests, and the number of young people, students and companies who have got in touch, wanting to get involved. Sometimes the guests have had so much fun that they cry at the end of the afternoon. Most touchingly, one elderly gentleman told me that he 'felt like a person again' after coming along to a few of the events. He had been given the opportunity to socialize and make new friends, something he hadn't done in a long time.

Remember Why You're Doing This

It is moments like these that never let me forget why I started this business in the first place. Having a sense of purpose, some kind of mental picture of where we're trying to get to, is the energy that fuels us through life. It might be material, wanting to live in a nice house with nice things.

But mostly we will have a desire to create something, make the people around us happy, be respected for building something worthwhile and having a positive impact on the world, making it a better place.

The key in all of this, as I touched on at the very start of the book, is asking yourself why. Why start a business at all?

A lot of the time, people behave one way in their personal lives and differently in business or at work. They have a different set of values in each place: buying free-range eggs at home but using battery ones in their restaurant, giving money to the homeless on a personal level but not responding to letters from charities that ask for help from their company.

I really think that an important point in life and in business is always to be true to what you believe in. A business should not be a machine, driven only by financial goals. It is a group of people who have come together to create value and meaning and hopefully to put something good out into the world.

Doing 'good' isn't necessarily about setting up a charity or giving away your profits to good causes. You do good simply by creating products that are worthwhile, that provide something of real value to people—making their lives a little better. You do good by creating jobs, giving other people a purpose in their lives. Of course, you can do a lot of good by creating a great place to work, making people happy and helping them to fulfil their own ambitions.

If you do good, giving something to people that they value, they will love you and your company for it. Your products will have meaning for them and they'll want to help you succeed. If you have a well-loved brand and a loyal customer base, you're going to be well placed to grow your business to even headier heights.

Environmental Activism: Patagonia (patagonia.com)

Patagonia, founded in 1972 by outdoor enthusiast Yvon Chouinard in California, has been a true pioneer of ethical business. Consistently ranked as one of the best employers in America, the company operates on flexi-time work hours, so that the staff can take time off to go surfing when the surf is good.

But where the company has really made an impact has been in its efforts to protect the environment and protest against environmental destruction. As a business, it commits to donating 1% of its sales or 10% of profits, whichever is greater, to environmental groups; so far it has donated over $25 million.

While Patagonia has done so much for the environment and ethical business, it has also become a commercially successful company in the process, employing over 1,200 people and with revenues exceeding $270 million. It demonstrates that it is not only possible to run a business ethically, but that customers will love you for it and reward you by buying your products, because they want to be part of your movement. Patagonia goes to huge lengths to reduce the impact of its own products on the environment and has been a beacon for other companies to follow on the road towards sustainability.

10 Building a Team

You may well have a loyal and enthusiastic customer base and big ambitions for the future, but there's a limit to how much you can continue to do on your own. Before you start trying to take over the world, you're going to have to build a team around you and a solid company culture. You're going to have to be sure that you have a solid base that you can build on and be confident that you can continue to keep your existing customers happy, even when you start wooing new ones.

Up until now you've probably done everything yourself, including the tasks that you don't enjoy quite as much. You've done most of the jobs in the business, from developing the product in the first place to making the tea at meetings. So the chances are, you end up spending most of your time working on tasks that don't create much value.

As your business grows, the demands on your time will become greater, and the key to your success will lie in figuring out what it is that your role in the business really is. Perhaps there is one area of the business that you most enjoy, say meeting with potential customers and telling them all about your concept. Or maybe you are most passionate when you are actively going out and selling your product, coming up with new ideas, or motivating your team. So if you want your company to grow, you're going to have to figure out how you can spend as much of your time as possible on the jobs that you most enjoy and that create the most value in your business. When you spend time on the part of your business that you are most passionate about, you do a great job of it and hopefully bring a lot of money into the business. This is the work with which you add the most value.

The key is to cut everything else out of your day: all of the menial tasks like answering the phone, sending out invoices and chasing up late payers, and the jobs you're not so good at. You can do that by employing a great team that you can delegate all of that work to, or by finding an outside company to do these tasks for you.

You will no doubt have to consider taking on the first members of your team, or building on the one you already have. This presents a whole range of challenges and the moment you take on your first employee, you take on a special set of responsibilities that you haven't yet had. Now you aren't merely responsible for your own career, it is down to you to keep your employee in work. The decisions you take as you grow the company will put their employment at risk. They are relying on you for their livelihood, their ability to pay the rent and support their family. Suddenly, things become a lot more serious.

Although employing people comes with responsibilities, it feels pretty amazing to start creating a team of people who can begin growing the company. Everyone who joins the team will be bringing their own set of experiences and ideas, sometimes very different to your own. The people you bring into your team are likely to be the ones interacting with your customers, which means it is crucial that you attract the right people to work with you. Their ability and enthusiasm for the job will have a huge effect on your business.

Attracting the Right People

So there's a fair chance that you will need to take on someone with experience to help you develop the company. There's a lot of sense in discovering the areas of your business that you're not good at, maybe finance or product development, and taking on someone who is a lot better than you to do those jobs.

In a conventional company when you want to recruit someone, you usually put an advert about it in the local newspaper or perhaps online. You try to find the person who is best qualified to do the job.

Although it is obviously important to take on employees who are qualified to do the jobs you need to get done, I don't think that is the only aspect to consider. You have to find someone who is going to fit your company, someone who gets what you're all about and buys into the bigger picture of where you are trying to take the business.

The people you need to attract to your team will depend on your type of business, the work that you are hoping to delegate and how much you can afford to pay for the first members of your team.

You might well consider taking on someone part-time to help out with some of the tasks that are eating up so much of your own time, like admin and finance. Or, if you don't have a lot of money available to employ people, you could look into taking on an intern.

Internships are commonplace in the design, fashion and music industries. Youngsters who are just getting started in the industry can take up an internship as a kind of apprenticeship, giving them the opportunity to learn and develop their skills. Because they don't have a great deal of experience, they will usually start an internship unpaid, with only their expenses being covered by the company. As they progress, the aim is that the company will get to a position of being able to offer them a full-time paid position.

At SuperJam we often have recent graduates applying to come and work with us. Currently we have a couple of design interns and one who is working on sales and marketing. They were all attracted to work with us after reading a job description on the site Enternships.com, which is a great place to find enterprising young interns to join your company. The interns gain a great deal of experience and have the opportunity to work in an entrepreneurial and fun company. As their host, the company benefits from their enthusiasm, ideas and the work they produce.

When I have been recruiting people for our company, I look at all of the people who are most passionate about SuperJam. The people who write about us on their blogs, tell all their friends about us, send in suggestions of new stores that we should be selling the products to and volunteer to help set up tea parties in their communities.

I'd go as far as to say that they are the people who love the brand. Some of them love it almost as much as I do. They're exactly the kind of people who should be working with me. Who better to sell your product than someone who buys it themselves and really believes in it?

SuperJam's Recruits

By finding people who are super passionate about our brand, I've managed to build a team who are really motivated and who love the work SuperJam does. They're a group of people who love jam, really enjoy telling people about our brand and get a lot of satisfaction from coming along to the tea parties, feeling that they are part of a business that has meaning.

About half a dozen people who work at SuperJam travel around supermarket stores, music festivals, food fairs and other big events, handing out samples and telling people about the products. They all do an amazing job of it. Not because they've had any experience of this kind of work before, but because they really care about SuperJam. In their spare time they help out at the tea parties and they are always on the look-out for more little shops that we should be selling to.

Everyone who works at SuperJam is encouraged to post their ideas or news onto the Facebook page, Twitter and blog to share with everyone else. They might talk about about how much fun they're having serving scones at a music festival or about a celebrity who has stopped by the camper van to say hi.

I'm sure you can imagine the value in fostering a sense of community and a sense that everyone in the company is connected. When everyone is connected in a company and knows where the business is trying to go, it becomes really easy to manage them. In fact, because everyone at SuperJam is so motivated about the work they're doing and understands what the brand is all about, it is really easy to let them more or less manage their own work.

Flexible Working

Some of the SuperJam team are musicians, some are artists and quite a few of them are students. They have lots of other exciting things going on in their lives aside from working with me and I have to embrace that. I want SuperJam to be a super flexible place to work, where people are not being micro-managed, somewhere without heaps of bureaucracy or procedures. I just want the customer to be happy and I figure that if the job in hand gets done, everyone is happy.

So how do I manage everyone? Well, in a lot of ways I'd say that everyone manages themselves. I don't dictate what work anyone does, what hours they work, how they do it. I want them to be independent, to come up with their own ideas and search out opportunities for themselves and the company.

We have a big Google calendar that everyone has access to, where they can pick what work to do and tell everyone what they're up to. Super simple. Obviously, if I were employing more people we'd use something more sophisticated. But it does the trick: I can post what stores we need to visit or where samples need to be handed out. One of the team might hear about a food fair that they think we should go to and can post it up there. They then collaborate with a couple of the other people to figure out what days they're going to work, how they're going to get there, how they're going to set everything up. If, for instance, someone can't work a particular day, they can communicate with some of the other team members and get one of them to visit the store in their place.

It probably sounds like chaos if you're used to working in a company where it is someone's job to manage a rota. But I think this is what my generation want their workplace to look like: they want to be able to manage their own time, spending time outside of work on the things that are important to them as well as working for the company they love when they wish to.

Although I'm sure you'll be able to find a great team of passionate people who love your products and do a great job of keeping your customers happy, there might be some jobs that you can't hire someone to do. Perhaps there are aspects of your business that aren't really core to what you do and you should think about finding a reliable external company to take care of them for you.

Outsourcing

Outsourcing can be something of a dirty word. It probably conjures up images of vast call centres in India filled with enthusiastic young operatives cold calling British housewives, interrupting *Eastenders* to try to sell them mobile phone contracts.

However, in reality outsourcing doesn't usually mean sending work overseas. Most of the time it is about companies finding someone else to do all of the tasks that aren't central to their business.

You would be amazed at what you can outsource to companies that can probably do a better, cheaper and more efficient job than you could do yourself. As you would imagine, there are companies that will answer your phone calls; so long as the person they have picking up the phone knows all about your brand, this can work really well. They'll be able to answer questions from your customers, respond to complaints and turn down pesky sales calls.

Usually it makes a lot of sense to outsource your accounting and bookkeeping. If you find a good company to work with, they'll be able to send out invoices to your customers, keep track of all of your expenses and maybe even chase up the customers who haven't paid on time. They will also, of course, deal with all of your tax and prepare your accounts at the end of the year.

In the US, there is a company called Earth Class Mail that offers small businesses a secure service of having all of their mail opened, scanned and emailed to them as an attachment. There's no need even to have a physical mailing address, as all of your mail is redirected to Earth Class Mail. This kind of service is ideal for entrepreneurs who travel a lot and also means that everything mailed to the company can be easily stored and accessed online. Although there isn't a similar service in the UK just yet, I've heard it won't be long before there is.

Of course, you might decide to outsource the manufacturing of your product or the delivery of your service, if this isn't a strong point of yours. You might feel that building a brand is where your passion lies, or in sales and marketing.

A massive range of businesses, from food brands like Innocent to technology companies like Apple and maybe even your local plumber, outsource their production or the delivery of their services. That's because they've decided that the job they're good at is developing products, finding customers and promoting their brand. It makes a lot of sense for them to find someone else to do the production, who will no doubt do a better or cheaper job than they could.

SuperJam's Manufacturing Partners

When you're looking for a manufacturing or service partner, there are all kinds of factors to consider. This isn't a relationship that you want to rush into; it could well be one of the most important decisions of your business career. If the partner turns out to not be as great as you had hoped, maybe delivering late or at a substandard quality, it could destroy your brand in no time.

You're going to need to see samples of other products it has produced and also have the company produce a test batch of your own product. If you're having another company deliver your service, perhaps consider giving it a trial run with a few of your customers and asking them for feedback.

In the case of working with a factory, you will want to visit it for yourself. Until you actually stand in the factory and see the machines and employees with your own eyes, you have no idea what the standards are, regardless of what the sales team tells you. For all you know, that sales team might turn out to be an intermediary as well.

Chinese Production

The pitfalls of setting up a relationship with a partner can be a particular problem when you are dealing with potential manufacturers in China or other low-cost countries. There will no doubt be concerns in your mind over the safety and conditions of the factory workers and the quality and integrity of the goods they produce.

Although all of the production of SuperJam takes place in the UK, we have relationships with great partners in other countries for the production of our branded aprons and homewares. I am sure that we would all love for everything we sell to be produced on our own shores, but the reality is that for some types of products it isn't easy to find a way of making that competitive.

You may well find yourself producing a product that is struggling to compete at its current price and you could be finding it difficult to make any decent margins. Locating a production partner overseas could reduce costs to a point where you're in a better position to offer a more competitive price, grow your business and end up creating a lot of well-paid jobs in product development and marketing in your community.

The internet has made the world a much smaller place and finding an overseas partner can be fairly straightforward and a lot less daunting than you might imagine. Sites like Alibaba.com list the thousands of manufacturers that are out there for every conceivable kind of product, from MP3 players to Halloween costumes and industrial freezers to syringes.

You can contact manufacturers of similar products to yours and send them some details about what you are looking for right away. From my experience, the companies in China are hungry for success and efficient beyond our usual expectations, sometimes responding to your enquiries within hours.

When you are dealing with overseas manufacturers there can be language and cultural barriers to overcome and both sides will have reservations about putting too much trust in someone from the other side of the world. I would suggest that you should do everything you can to make your requirements extremely clear. Always send a sample or prototype of what you are looking for them to produce and ask them to replicate it and send their version back to you.

Whether your manufacturing partner is in the UK or elsewhere, over time you will build a relationship with them. You'll become more and more trusting of one another and hopefully will be able to work closely together to develop new products and improve what you are offering to your customers.

Crowdsourcing

Sometimes there are jobs that are being done in your company that could be done by your customers or by the public. It probably sounds a bit strange, but what is sometimes called 'crowdsourcing' is really transforming whole industries. If you think about the music industry, it is traditionally someone's job to find new talent and pick which acts should get signed to a record label. But now people like Simon Cowell, with shows such as the *The X Factor*, have turned that on its head. The public finds the new acts by voting for the ones they think should make it. Of course, sometimes the acts they pick don't set the world on fire, but on the whole the public chooses the act that is most likely to have commercial success.

I love the idea that we can let the people who buy our products, the public, to get involved in the company and collaborate with one another to help SuperJam grow. We can ask them for ideas for new products or suggestions of new stores that we could be supplying to.

An idea that I am really excited about is letting consumers organize tea parties completely independently of SuperJam. We can let them collaborate with one another on Facebook, Twitter and our website and once they have found a venue, elderly people from their local community and a few people to help out at the party, we will give them a grant, something like £100, to host the party. They'll be encouraged to upload videos of the event onto the web, take lots of pictures and promote it on our Facebook page.

You can probably imagine how many tea parties we could run if we make it really easy for the people who love SuperJam and who are passionate about the tea parties idea to host their own parties in their own communities. We have had about 50 events like this so far and once we figure out exactly how to put it all together, we could have hundreds, probably thousands of events happening all over the country, with tens of thousands of elderly people coming along and having a fun time.

I think that is pretty amazing. By getting the people who love SuperJam to help us out with information about stores we should be supplying, ideas for new products or even giving their time in helping to organize tea parties, we actually get a lot of work done that otherwise we'd need to employ someone to do.

Whether you bring enthusiastic new talent into your business, find outside companies to take over some of your workload or encourage your customers to help you grow your business, you'll find that having a strong team around you puts you in a great position to start developing your business and taking advantage of all of the new ideas that present themselves.

11 Diversify and Grow

Once you're a superstar in the market that you have started out selling your product in and have a built a strong team in your business, you will be in a great position to take advantage of all of the opportunities ahead. You will no doubt start to broaden your horizons and think about all of the opportunities that are out there for your brand. This might involve going to new markets or new countries and maybe even coming up with some great ideas for how you can extend your brand into entirely new products.

Over the past four or five years, SuperJam has gone from only selling a couple of flavours of jam to offering a much wider range of products, and even selling things that aren't jam at all, such as books, aprons and gift sets. Not only have we broadened the range of products we sell, but we've taken our brand to new retailers and even overseas.

Finding New Markets

There will be all sorts of new places that you can search out to sell your products to. The reputation and experience that you have built up so far will stand you in good stead to take your brand to a bigger and more diverse range of customers.

Diversifying your brand might mean a number of things. It could simply mean adding more varieties to your range, offering your core product in a wider range of flavours, colours, sizes or packages, or in ways that make it more appealing at different times of year or to different groups of people. You might add a Christmas version or a Kosher option, for instance. You could work your way into other industries or the public sector simply by repackaging what you offer. By exploring different options like this, you can find entirely new outlets for your product that may not have been so obvious at first.

You could also consider what extra functions or services your customers ask for and develop a premium version of your core product to which your most die-hard fans are likely to upgrade. In the same kind of way, you might want to simplify your product and offer a budget option for consumers who can't access your brand at its current price.

There's a whole world out there filled with people who will love your product. You simply need a plan and some good support around you to figure out how to get it to them.

Diversifying the SuperJam Range

When I first started selling jam, I didn't imagine that I would end up seeing the SuperJam brand on anything other than jars of jam.

However, over the past few years I have been open to experimenting with new product ideas and we now have a whole range of kitchenware, including aprons, tea towels and totes, gift boxes, teapots, cake stands and all kinds of other products that are related to jam and afternoon tea.

By continually launching new products, we are able to keep our customers excited about the brand and it gives us a good excuse to keep in contact with the buyers at the big retailers.

I'm not very sure how far we could extend the SuperJam brand, but it makes sense that we should develop quality food-related products, such as like peanut butter, honey, curds and marmalades. There's no reason to say that one day we couldn't launch our own branded toaster or jam-making equipment.

I've got ideas to launch a range of jams specifically for kids, and to package SuperJam in tiny little jars to go on airplanes and hotel breakfast tables.

I really love coming up with new ideas for products that we can create. I'm sure that you'll be excited to see your brand extend into new areas too. What is most important is to make sure that what you offer to your customers is something you are proud of, that it ties in with your brand and is a worthwhile product. Otherwise, you could end up overstretching your brand and doing it a great deal of damage.

Making the leap from being a small company to a medium one is a point at which so many businesses fail. This might be because they risk all of their resources on an entirely new product, or they find that their brand isn't as well suited to life in a foreign country as they hoped it would be. Many entrepreneurs take their eye off the ball as their business grows, losing their grip on what really matters: their core product and the first few customers who brought them to where they are now.

Don't Stretch Your Brand too Far

I'm a huge believer in experimenting and, every now and again, trying out a crazy idea just to see what might happen.

Opening our own stores, dedicated to selling SuperJam, gift sets and a few related high-end food products, was one of those ideas. In 2009, during a recession, against the background of the closure of Woolworths and hundreds of other stores, landlords of commercial property were desperate to get people to open up in their boarded-up shops.

We were approached by a shopping centre in Aberdeen that had some empty space and offered us the chance to try it out at no cost, no strings attached, to open up SuperJam's first store.

It was quite an exciting experience. I found a few staff to work in the tiny little shop, put up signs and got some local press on the day we opened.

Business started out quite well, with lots of initial interest and we sold plenty of jars of jam. But sadly, the store struggled to make any money by the time the costs were covered and I decided to end the experiment after just a few weeks.

It seemed that the idea of opening a shop dedicated to selling jam was a step too far. Perhaps if we had a wider range and some more higher-margin products, like gift sets, it could have worked.

I was glad to have given it a shot and, who knows, maybe we'll come back to the idea of opening our own stores somewhere down the line. But for now, that was one of those ideas that just didn't work.

Going International

Much of the time you don't need to come up with crazy ideas for new products or new ways to sell your brand at all. There are all sorts of ways in which you can sell the same product but in different places, maybe even abroad. You could try getting your products into more stores in your country to start with, franchising your concept to other entrepreneurs in different areas or targeting a new niche of the market by working with specialist distributors.

In the case of SuperJam, it seemed obvious that, given the success of the brand in the UK, we could probably have a shot at doing the same overseas. What has really amazed me over the past few years has been the way in which the SuperJam story has travelled much further than the products have, even further than I have for that matter.

The story of the wee Scottish guy who got his gran's jam into big supermarkets has been covered on the largest news show in China, in newspapers in Canada and in documentaries about young entrepreneurs in Taiwan. SuperJam is used as a case study in business textbooks in Denmark and to teach kids English in Russia.

Of course, because of the media coverage, supermarket chains all over the world have got in touch, expressing an interest in stocking SuperJam. We've had approaches from up-market department stores in Dubai to some of the largest chains in the United States.

Initially, it was very difficult for me to follow up all of these enquiries. Not only were there language barriers, I didn't know technically how to export the products.

Although we have taken orders from the far corners of the world, SuperJam is not on sale in many outlets outside of the UK. The biggest barrier to our growth in foreign markets so far has been having a lack of local knowledge and contacts. I've figured out that the way to grow into each country is to find a local distributor to contact stores, get orders, market the brand and try to get press coverage for the story.

Although there can be many barriers to getting your product established in an international market, the rewards can be huge. As with every new venture, there's a lot to be said for starting small, giving it a shot and seeing what happens. One day, your product could be the next big thing in a foreign country you haven't even visited yet.

The Future and Beyond

If I look back at SuperJam's humble beginnings in my parents' tiny kitchen in Edinburgh, I can barely believe where it has ended up.

I know that the 14-year-old me would never believe it if you told him. I don't think anyone could imagine that what started out as a hobby and a few empty old jars could grow into a company supplying the biggest supermarket chains in the world.

What my story shows is that what starts as a hobby in a kitchen, garage, bedroom or garden shed, with a bit of love and hard work and support from people around you, can grow into something amazing. Something that changes a life. I know that SuperJam has not just changed my life, it has also created a livelihood for a lot of people and has had a positive impact on communities.

If I imagine how far SuperJam has come in these few years, I can't even begin to guess how far it can go in the future.

Launching new flavours and products is part of its future, as is launching in countries all around the world. But what is exciting for me is that it will involve all kinds of things that we haven't even thought of yet.

As long as I stay open to new ideas and opportunities, SuperJam can go as far and as wide as my imagination will take it. As for your own adventure, if you open your mind to new ideas and are willing to give anything a shot, you could well be amazed at where your journey will end up.

A Handful of Places to Go for Inspiration

Support Organizations

♦ **The Prince's Trust (PSYBT in Scotland)**—It offers grants, loans, advice and mentoring to hundreds of young people setting up in business every year.

Websites

♦ **Shell-Livewire.org**—Advice for start-up entrepreneurs, grants and an annual Young Entrepreneur of the Year competition. Check out the online discussion forums, where you can talk about your ideas with other people starting out in business.

♦ **Springwise.com**—This site features innovative new start-ups from around the world and is a frequent source of inspiration.

♦ **Trendspotting.com**—This site comments on trends in society with a view to them being inspiration for business ideas.

- **PSFK.com**—A site about trends, new ideas and innovations from around the world.
- **Smarta.com**—Advice, interviews with entrepreneurs and information about grant funding.
- **Coolhunting.com**—Cool new products from all over the world.
- **Startups.co.uk**—This site has a discussion forum, interviews with entrepreneurs and several competitions that you might be eligible to enter.

Books

- **A Book about Innocent** (Michael Joseph, 2009)—The story of how the founders built Innocent into a £100 m+ brand.
- **Ben & Jerry's Double Dip** (Simon & Schuster, 1999)—The story of Ben Cohen and Jerry Greenfield.
- **Business as Unusual** (Anita Roddick Books, 2005)—Anita Roddick's book on using business as protest and a way of bringing about social change.
- **Crush It!** (HarperBusiness, 2009)—Gary Vaynerchuck's story of Wine TV and how you can use social media and the web to promote your business and your personal brand.
- **Delivering Happiness** (Business Plus, 2010)—The story of Zappos.com and its founder, Tony Hseih. How he built a $1 billion online retailer selling shoes with the help of a great company culture and amazing customer service.

- **Good to Great** (Random House Business, 2001)—Jim Collins investigates why some companies make the leap and become great, while others don't.
- **Raising the Bar** (Jossey Bass, 2004)—The story of Clif Bar, a cool and ethical company that makes snack bars for athletes.

Index

Innocent 12, 25, 70, 71, 146, 148, 170, 184
innovation 23, 31, 143
inspiration 12, 17, 19, 22, 31, 140, 146, 183, 184
International 88, 148, 152, 180, 181
internet 18, 45, 115, 116, 124, 140, 172
Interviews 95, 184
investors 42, 46, 57, 59, 150, 155
Labeling 36, 73

L
Launch 24, 45, 46, 52, 60, 65, 76–78, 79, 81–91, 102, 113, 120, 137, 138, 178
Launch Party 84
Letters 114, 134–136, 139, 152, 158
loans 42, 183
Love 2, 5, 6, 12, 16, 17, 19, 23, 25, 30, 31, 34, 38, 42, 45–47, 61, 63, 65, 71, 73, 78, 80, 82, 87, 92, 98, 99, 100, 103, 107, 116, 122, 126, 129–132, 135–139, 142, 144, 149, 158, 159, 165, 166, 168, 171, 173, 174, 177, 178, 182
Loyalty 127, 128, 150

M
Manufacturing 78, 170, 172
Market Research 22, 54

marketing 24, 56, 63, 111, 113, 115, 121, 136, 138, 139, 146, 165, 170, 172
mentors 39
Millionaire 11, 142
motivation 7, 11, 12
MyMuesli 28

N
Newspapers 87, 90, 94, 102, 110–112, 164, 180
Non-Executive Director 41

O
Online Advertising 115, 116
Outlets 53, 102, 139, 177, 181
Outsourcing 168, 169

P
Packaging 24, 25, 64, 68, 70–73, 79, 80, 136, 146
Partnerships 122, 123
Patagonia 12, 146, 159
People 2, 3, 4, 8, 9, 11–13, 16–18, 20–31, 34–40, 42, 45–47, 51–54, 56, 57, 59–63, 68, 69, 76–80, 82–85, 87, 88, 90–93, 95–100, 103–119, 121–124, 126, 127, 129–140, 142–159, 163–168, 173, 174, 177, 179, 182, 183
Pitching 50, 59, 60, 61, 67, 103, 104
PR Agency 87, 88